Case Studies of Openness in the Language Classroom

Edited by Ana Beaven, Anna Comas-Quinn and Barbara Sawhill

Published by Research-publishing.net
Dublin, Ireland; Voillans, France
info@research-publishing.net

Typeset by Research-publishing.net
Cover design: © Raphaël Savina (raphael@savina.net)

Fonts used are licensed under a SIL Open Font License

ISBN13: 978-1-908416-09-4 (Paperback, Print on Demand, Lulu.com)
ISBN13: 978-1-908416-10-0 (Ebook, PDF file, Open Access, Research-publishing.net)
ISBN13: 978-1-908416-11-7 (Ebook, Kindle Edition, Amazon Media EU S.à r.l.)

British Library Cataloguing-in-Publication Data.
A cataloguing record for this book is available from the British Library.

Bibliothèque Nationale de France - Dépôt légal: septembre 2013.

Table of Contents

Section 3. Sharing Practice

Section 4. Collaborative Learning & Student-generated Content

Section 5. Learner Autonomy

Notes on Contributors

Editors

Ana Beaven works at the University of Bologna Language Centre (Italy), where she teaches general English as well as English for Academic Purposes. Her research interests are in the fields of intercultural communication, language teaching and assessment, and the use of technology in the language classroom. She has taken part in various European projects: WebCEF (www. webcef.eu) and CEFcult (www.cefcult.eu), which developed tools for the assessment of oral skills, Performing Languages (www.performinglanguages. eu), dealing with the application of drama techniques to foreign language teaching, and is coordinator of the IEREST project (www.ierest-project.eu), for the development of intercultural resources for Erasmus students and their teachers.

Anna Comas-Quinn is a Lecturer in Spanish at the Department of Languages, at The Open University, UK, and a Teaching Fellow for the Support Centre for Open Resources in Education (SCORE). She led the development of LORO (http://loro.open.ac.uk), an open repository of teaching resources for language teachers and learners, and has researched and published in the area of technology-enhanced language learning, mobile language learning, teacher development, and open educational resources and practices. She is also interested in the potential of openness for professional development, and has worked to embed open practices in several projects ranging from the collaborative writing of teaching materials, to the application of drama techniques to language teaching (www.performinglanguages.eu), or the exploration of Open Translation tools and practices (www.ot12.org).

Barbara Sawhill is the Director of the Cooper International Learning Center and a Lecturer in Hispanic Studies at Oberlin College (Oberlin, OH, USA), positions she has held since 1998. Prior to her position at Oberlin, she taught Spanish and directed a language resource center at the pre-university level. Her research interests include the use of blogging, social media, and student self-assessment in language teaching and learning. Author of several articles about the use of social tools and self assessment in language teaching, Barbara is the

Past President of IALLT (http://iallt.org). She is a frequent invited presenter at professional conferences, and the lead author for Language Lab Unleashed! (http://languagelabunleashed.org), a blog dedicated to exploring appropriate and effective uses of technology in the language classroom.

Authors

Carl Blyth is an applied linguist with a background in pragmatics and technology and an emphasis on cross-cultural and intercultural interaction. Currently, he is working on an analysis of online dialogues from the Cultura archive, a telecollaboration between French and American universities. Blyth's professional interests also include the use of digital tools and social media to facilitate collaborative social action, with a particular emphasis on textual annotation software for social reading. Working with departmental colleagues and graduate students he created a suite of online pedagogical materials for French (e.g. Tex's French Grammar, a pedagogical reference grammar; and Français interactif, a blended learning environment for beginning French). He is the Director of the Center for Open Educational Resources and Language Learning (COERLL), a foreign language resource center funded by the US Department of Education. COERLL's mission is to produce and disseminate OERs for the Internet public.

Kate Borthwick is an academic coordinator for e-learning at the Centre for Languages, Linguistics and Area Studies (LLAS) based at the University of Southampton, UK. She is an experienced developer of online learning materials and an e-tutor and currently coordinates LLAS activity in relation to the use of technology in language teaching and learning, initiating and managing projects, devising and delivering training, and organising and running events, notably the Centre's annual e-learning symposium. She manages the development and training for the LOC tool (an online authoring tool developed at LLAS), and also manages two online teaching and learning repositories hosted by LLAS (*LanguageBox* and *HumBox*). She has managed all of the Centre's recent projects exploring Open Educational Practice (*The*

HumBox Project 2009-10; *Community Café* 2010-2011; *FAVOR* 2011-2012, and *OpenLIVES* 2011-2013) and speaks regularly on the topic of open practice in language education at conferences and other events. She has a background in teaching English to international students across the globe and at universities in the UK.

Todd Bryant is the academic technology liaison to the foreign language departments at Dickinson College, Carlisle, Pennsylvania, US, and periodic instructor for the German department. He focuses on connecting language learners with native speakers via The Mixxer (www.language-exchanges.org) and other forms of social media. He has also used and written about games in education including "World of Warcraft" as an immersive environment for a German language course and using "Civilization IV" as a way of demonstrating systems level thinking in the social sciences.

Anna Calvi works as an Associate Lecturer, Teacher Trainer, Consultant and Author and specialises in English for Academic Purposes and Italian. She has an honours Open Degree from The Open University, a Master in English for Academic Purposes from Warwick University, a Postgraduate Diploma in Online and Distance Education from The Open University as well as the CELTA (Certificate in English Language Teaching to Adults) and the DELTA (Diploma in English Language Teaching to Adults- Modules 1 and 2). She has been teaching Italian as a Foreign Language for 10 years at the Warwick University Language Centre and for 7 years at The Open University. She has written paper and online materials for Italian, French and EAP courses. She is currently co-writing the new edition of *Andante*, the OU Beginners' Italian textbook.

Marco Cappellini is a PhD student in the research team STL (Savoirs, Textes, Langage - UMR 8163 CNRS) at Lille 3 University, France. He graduated in 2010, having researched scaffolding in a Teletandem environment for French and Chinese as foreign languages. He has worked in language teaching and teacher education at Lille 3 University (France) and at the Dalian University of Foreign Languages (China). His research focuses on learner autonomy, tandem language learning and computer-mediated communication for language learning.

Alison Dickens is currently Assistant Director of the Centre for Languages, Linguistics and Area Studies (LLAS), based at the University of Southampton, UK, responsible for the Higher Education dimension of its activities: the programme of training for staff, resource and course development, income generation and project work. She has directed or co-directed 3 EU funded projects: *Opening the Door to Language Learning* (2002-2005), *The Language Café* (2006-2008), *LanQua* (2007-2010) as well as directed projects in the fields of e-learning/Open Education Resources (*The HumBox Project* 2009-10; *Community Café* 2010-2011; *FAVOR* 2011-2012, and *OpenLIVES* 2011-2013). She has a background in language teaching and has worked in primary and secondary schools as well as in the HE sector for the past 17 years. She is a founder member of LLAS and with the small core team has built up a thriving and respected centre with a reputation for delivering high quality training, resources and advice to the languages and linguistics community in Higher Education.

Annette Duensing is a Senior Lecturer at The Open University, UK, and is responsible for the academic line-management and teacher development of a team of part-time teachers supporting students studying languages in the East of England region of the university. Annette has studied and taught Open University modules herself, and has extensive experience in developing language and language-related study materials. Outside The Open University she has been an author and academic editor for a number of language textbooks for different publishers. Annette conducts scholarship into students' perception of supported online learning and teacher development for this context, and has contributed to scholarly publications on blended teaching and learning, for instance as a co-author of a chapter on assessment in *Teaching Languages in Blended Contexts* (Murphy, Nicolson, & Southgate, eds., 2011).

Matilde Gallardo is a Senior Lecturer in the Department of Languages at The Open University, UK, where she has academic line-management and teacher-development responsibilities for the team of language teachers in the South East region. Matilde has extensive experience of MFL teacher professional development and has carried out scholarly activity and research into motivating factors of online collaboration and teachers' perceptions of their professional identity in blended contexts. She has led a joint online project for teachers of Spanish with the University of Córdoba, Spain, and more recently she has coordinated a collaborative staff development project on Dyslexia and Modern Language Learning. Her interests are in the field of collaborative online peer support and professional development in Open Educational Practices. She is co-author of the section on teacher development in *Teaching Languages in Blended Contexts* (Murphy, Nicolson, & Southgate, eds., 2011).

Dr Cecilia Goria is a Lecturer in Italian at the Language Centre, School of Cultures, Languages and Area Studies, University of Nottingham, UK. She has a PhD in Linguistics and is the author of *Subject Clitics in the Northern Italian Dialects: a comparative study based on the Minimalist Program and Optimality Theory* (Kluwer Academic Publisher 2004). Cecilia teaches Italian and Linguistics, and directs a postgraduate Masters degree in Digital Technologies for Language Teaching. In 2010, she obtained an MSc in eLearning at the University of Edinburgh and since then technology enhanced language learning and teaching is the focus of Cecilia's practice as well as her research. Specifically, Cecilia is currently investigating the theoretical implications and the pedagogical affordances and limitations of open courses within the context of language teaching.

Sarah Heiser is a Lecturer in the Department of Languages at The Open University, UK. She is based at The Open University in London and is responsible for the academic line-management and teacher development of the London languages team of part-time teachers. Her interests include Open Educational Resources and Open Educational Practices (OER/OEP), staff development by experiential learning in online spaces, student strategies for language learning and young students in Higher Education. She has been an active member of the Department of Languages VLE group. She is co-author of the section on teacher development in *Teaching Languages in Blended Contexts* (Murphy, Nicolson, & Southgate, eds., 2011).

María Dolores Iglesias Mora has been working as an Associate Lecturer of Spanish with The Open University for the last eleven years teaching courses from Beginners to Upper Intermediate levels. She holds an MA in Teaching English for International Business from the University of Central Lancashire and has collaborated in several projects about open educational resources and teaching practice. She has worked as a Spanish Lecturer at the University of Central Lancashire on a part time basis, as well as previously holding different management positions as Language Coordinator and Head of Languages in several institutions. Although a Spanish specialist, she has also taught English as a Foreign Language, and Study Skills for university students. In Spain she worked with corporate clients at the Spanish Ministry of Development, Alcatel and Robert Bosch companies. In Japan, she taught undergraduate and postgraduate university students and collaborated in the publication of a Spanish textbook for Beginners students. She is actively engaged in producing her own educational resources and has published some of them in LORO.

After a career of teaching and management in secondary schools, **Terry King** is currently a Research Associate in the School of European Languages, Culture and Society (SELCS) at University College London (UCL). His particular interest is in motivating school students to continue the study of languages at university. He manages the ATLAS, CROSSROADS, NEARPEERS and ONSTREAM projects. The first encourages school students to learn a new language at University, the second and third use a VLE to link pupils in secondary schools with undergraduates and teachers of the target language. The ONSTREAM project facilitates on-line collaboration between teachers of Russian in three sectors, HE, secondary and supplementary schools. From 2001 to 2011, he worked as a Research Fellow in the Centre for the Advancement of Teaching and Learning at UCL, attracting funding from a range of external sources. In addition, funded by an ESRC small award, he has conducted research into factors affecting recruitment to HE courses in the less widely taught languages and, for UCL, investigated its Personal Tutoring system. He has published in *ReCALL* and the *Language Learning Journal* and contributed a chapter to the book *Telecollaboration 2.0* (2010).

David Elvis Leeming has been a Senior Lecturer at the University of Central Lancashire in the School of Language, Literature, and International Studies for the past ten years. He leads an undergraduate degree in International Business Communication. He has a great deal of experience of working with students from a multicultural environment, and has taught in Greece and Japan. David holds an Executive MBA as well as an MA in Teaching English for International Business and an MSc in Multimedia Computing. He is also working toward a Professional Doctorate in Elite Performance and is MBTI step one qualified, Belbin Team Roles accredited, and the Richard Lewis Intercultural Communication model accredited. He is a Fellow of the Higher Education Academy. His research interests revolve around Intercultural Communication specifically team work and leadership. He is also interested in how to embed blended learning within global programmes.

Antonio Martínez-Arboleda (*Licenciado en Derecho*, MA Business Law, FHEA) is Principal Teaching Fellow in Spanish at the School of Modern Languages and Cultures at the University of Leeds. He began his career in language teaching at the Instituto Cervantes and the University of Leeds in 1998, as he was furthering his postgraduate studies in UK Law and Politics. In 1999 he introduced a module on Spanish Politics and started to teach Spanish in an Economic and Business context in the University of Leeds programme. In 2002 he designed the Autonomous Learning Portfolio currently used in Spanish and other languages at his institution. From 2002 to 2009, he created a range of resources for the development of academic skills through professional simulations, often using e-learning and group activities. In 2009, he commenced his work on Open Educational Resources as part of the HumBox Team. In 2011 he was awarded a SCORE fellowship to work on OER review by employers and became co-researcher of the JISC funded project OpenLIVES on digitised Life Stories. He is a member of the JORUM UK Steering Group and has been heavily involved in the design of the University of Leeds OER institutional policy.

Anna Motzo is an Associate Lecturer, Consultant and Author and is the Italian Language Coach at the Royal Academy of Music in London. She has a Degree in Philosophy from the University of Rome (Italy) and a PGCE from the Institute of Education (London). She has spent more than ten years teaching Italian to international students both in Italy and in the UK. Her main area of interest is devising and developing learning materials. Since joining the OU in 2007, she has become more interested in e-learning and has taken part in various projects including most recently one focusing on the implications of designing digital resources for learners with dyslexia. She is Member of the Italian Committee (Association for Language Learning). She is currently co-writing the new edition of *Andante*, the OU Beginners' Italian textbook.

Irina Nelson is a Senior Teaching Fellow in Spanish at the University of Southampton. She studied at King's College London. She has an MA in Latin American Studies from the Institute of Latin American Studies, University of London and an MA in Translation Studies from the University of Westminster. She is a member of the Institute of Translation and Interpreting (ITI) and a professional translator for the Areas of Media, Sustainable Development and the Environment. She has worked at the University of Southampton since 2001 and since the implementation of Southampton's VLE in 2003, she has been involved in the production of learning materials in a digital form in order to foster language acquisition. She has used different technologies to make accessible text, audio, video and testing exercises. She was one of the partners in the JISC-funded OpenLIVES project. As part of this project, she created a suite of interactive learning objects on the topic of oral history, which she has published as OERs, and which she makes use of with her students. Her students were heavily involved in OpenLIVES project activities and she continues to encourage students to create open digital content as part of their language learning.

Alicia Pozo-Gutiérrez is a Lecturer in Spanish Social and Political Studies at the Department of Modern Languages, University of Southampton. She has a PhD from the University of Southampton. Using oral history and ethnographic methods, she researches exile and migration in the Spanish-speaking world, with a focus on return migration in times of social and political change. She researched the life histories of former Basque evacuee children from the Spanish Civil War in Britain and she is currently working on the project 'From Transition to Crisis: An Oral History of Democratic Spain'. She teaches courses on Spanish social and political history, and transnational studies at undergraduate and postgraduate level. She was a partner on the JISC-funded OpenLIVES project and was the contributor of the original research data used as the basis for the project. This data consisted of audio interview recordings with Spanish migrants, and it was collected for a research project called 'Tales of Return,' which took place in 2008. The OpenLIVES project gave Alicia the opportunity to extend the life of the data she had collected, which would have otherwise been archived out of public view, and to reach new audiences.

Klaus-Dieter Rossade is Lecturer in German and currently Director of the Language Studies Programme at the Faculty of Education and Language Studies (FELS) at The Open University, UK. For the last 15 years, he has produced distance learning teaching and learning materials, including open educational resources and designed language and culture courses in German at all levels. His research interests include the fields of intercultural communication and technology enhanced language learning. His PhD research focussed on the history of German Studies, intellectuals in totalitarian systems and questions relating to memory and 'dealing with the past'. He is a Fellow of the Higher Education Academy in the UK.

Sandra Silipo works as an Associate Lecturer, Consultant and Author for The Open University, UK. She has a Degree in Classics from the University of Turin (Italy) and an MA in Applied Linguistics from the University of East Anglia (Norwich, UK). She qualified in 1995 as Teacher of Italian as a Foreign Language (University of Siena for Foreigners, Italy) and as a Teacher of Foreign Languages to Adults in 2000 (RSA TFLA Diploma) while working as a Curriculum Support Tutor for the Languages Department of the Norfolk Adult Education Service. She has been teaching Italian as a Foreign Language for the past 20 years, both online and face-to-face. She is the co-author of *Colloquial Italian 2* for the Routledge Colloquial 2 series (Lymbery & Silipo,

Colloquial Italian 2, Routledge, 2003) and of *L150 Vivace* (© The Open University 2011). She is also currently co-writing the new edition of *Andante*, the OU Beginners' Italian textbook.

Julie Watson is Principal Teaching Fellow in e-Learning and Head of eLanguages in Modern Languages at the University of Southampton. She has an extensive background in directing and teaching EFL/EAP courses in the UK and overseas. She moved into the field of e-learning in 2001 and has been involved in a range of projects involving new technologies since then. She designed and led the development of the Prepare for Success website for international students, and led the design of the LOC authoring tool, the development of eLanguages Toolkits and a range of online courses, including the MA in ELT: Online. She has been involved in several OER projects and more recently, in researching digital literacies and developing a MOOC. Her main research interests are learning design, the implementation of new technologies in language learning, and online tutoring.

Susanne Winchester is an Associate Lecturer in German at The Open University, UK, and has over 20 years experience as a teacher, examiner, curriculum coordinator and teacher trainer in secondary, further and higher education. She is the author of Talk German 2 in the BBC Active Series. In recent years, she has developed a keen interest in technology enhanced language learning and teaching, in particular task-based learning in virtual worlds. She is currently working on research for a Doctorate in Education (EdD) qualification at The Open University, examining the use of electronic vocabulary training programmes for vocabulary learning.

Acknowledgements

The authors would like to thank the following organizations for their support during the creation of this book:

- European Association for Computer-Assisted Language Learning (EUROCALL) http://www.eurocall-languages.org/

- Università di Bologna, Italy http://www.unibo.it/it

- The Office of the Dean of the College of Arts and Sciences at Oberlin College (Oberlin, OH USA) http://new.oberlin.edu/office/dean-of-the-college-of-arts-and-sciences/

- The Open University, UK http://www.open.ac.uk

Ana Beaven, Anna Comas-Quinn and Barbara Sawhill

Foreword

The book you have before you is in line with one of the most democratic movements brought about thanks to the Internet; the elimination of access barriers in order to share research-related literature in hope that this will "lay the foundation for uniting humanity in a common intellectual conversation and quest for knowledge" regardless of wealth, location and opportunities. These words are from the Budapest Open Access Initiative[1], which marked the beginning of the Open Access movement. In the field of higher education, however, there was an earlier initiative led by the Massachusetts Institute of Technology (MIT) in the USA. MIT launched its Open Courseware (OCW)[2] programme in 2001, consisting of a web-based publication of virtually all MIT course content, having grown from barely 50 in-house courses to a current 2150 courses delivered by 250 institutions worldwide open to any interested party and freely available from their website.

These two examples strike me as being the ideal framework for this book… a) because it is freely distributed to language teachers throughout and b) because of the generosity of the practitioners and researchers who have contributed to this publication, and who are willing to share with the language learning and teaching community at large their work and expertise.

Congratulations to all!!

Ana Gimeno-Sanz
Universidad Politécnica de Valencia, Spain

---

1 Available from http://www.budapestopenaccessinitiative.org/read

2 More information available from http://ocw.mit.edu

Introduction on Case Studies
of Openness in the Language Classroom

Ana Beaven[1], Anna Comas-Quinn[2] and Barbara Sawhill[3]

---

1.   Project background

The last ten years have seen a considerable increase in the sharing of resources and practices in education, mainly based on the huge potential that online technologies and the internet have for making knowledge available openly (Pantò & Comas-Quinn, 2013). The shift now is from an interest in Open Educational Resources (OER), defined as "materials used to support education that may be freely accessed, reused, modified and shared by anyone" (Downes, 2011), to the realisation that openness itself, rather than the resources alone, can bring enormous benefits to the education community. Hence the focus on Open Educational Practices (OEP) defined as practices which "support the production, use and reuse of high quality OER through institutional policies, which promote innovative pedagogical models, and respect and empower learners as co-producers on their lifelong learning path" (ICDE, 2011).

Beyond the abundance of information that is available via the Internet, and the possibility of sharing and reusing resources, the web also offers huge opportunities to create connections for learning. This has great potential to transform education, as easy access to information, and the possibility of learning from others outside the classroom make teaching less hierarchical, thus disrupting the traditional pedagogical paradigms.In the specific case of language teaching and learning, this profusion of information and connections facilitate a more authentic use of

1. Università di Bologna, Italy; anamaria.beaven@unibo.it

2. The Open University, UK; anna.comas-quinn@open.ac.uk

3. Oberlin College, Oberlin, OH, USA; barbara.sawhill@oberlin.edu

How to cite this chapter: Beaven, A. Comas-Quinn, A., & Sawhill, B. (2013). Introduction on Case Studies of Openness in the Language Classroom. In A. Beaven, A. Comas-Quinn, & B. Sawhill (Eds), *Case Studies of Openness in the Language Classroom* (pp. 1-8). © Research-publishing.net.

---

the target language as well as contact with different cultures through accessing online text and audio-visual material in every language, as well as existing online communities. Clearly, this requires both teachers and learners to engage with language teaching and learning in novel ways.

In addition, open access initiatives to make research publications freely available online or the adoption of open source software solutions are already impacting education at all levels worldwide. For example, teachers and learners can make their voices heard and can create an online presence in the discipline through online publishing, be it in blogs, forums, through repositories, webpages, etc. Many language teachers already contribute to their discipline by sharing resources and ideas through online repositories such as Merlot, Connexions, Humbox or LORO, or in online communities such as mfltwitterati or the Guardian's Teacher Network.

The present publication arose from the two-day conference "Learning through Sharing: Open Resources, Open Practices, Open Communication" organised jointly by the EUROCALL Teacher Education and Computer Mediated Communication Special Interest Groups at the University of Bologna (Italy) on 29-30 March 2012 (http://eurocallsigsbologna.weebly.com). The main objective was to showcase the many ways in which practitioners in different settings are engaging with the concepts of open resources and practices, and to provide ideas for language teachers who might want to dip their toes into the OER/OEP world, or experiment further.

2.　　Contents and audience

This collection of case studies is addressed specifically to practitioners, foreign and second language teachers both in secondary and tertiary education. These are not research papers, although research certainly was essential in the creation of many of the projects these studies describe. Rather, they are short, directed descriptions of tools, projects, or activities with concrete examples of ways for teachers to consider using them in their practice. To make it simpler for readers to find examples of openness that are relevant to them, the case studies have been organised into five sections dealing with open tools for collaboration, sharing resources, sharing practices, collaborative learning and student-generated content, and learner autonomy.

2.1.   Open tools for collaboration

Sawhill opens the section on collaborative tools with an interesting case study on the implementation of an open blogging tool adapted to the needs of the language classroom. This provides a central page that aggregates the information from learners' blogs to make it easier for the teacher to monitor blogging activity and comment on others' contributions. Through a series of examples, Sawhill illustrates how a tool that facilitates the effective integration of blogs in language learning can encourage teachers and their learners to connect with the outside world and become part of authentic conversations with target language speakers.

Facilitating communication and enabling connections between speakers of different languages is also the purpose of The Mixxer, a platform described by Bryant in the second case study, which currently boasts over 100,000 users representing over 100 languages. This free, flexible platform for learners and teachers allows them to connect with native speakers on either an individual or class-to-class basis, making it possible for students to engage in synchronous, real time exchanges to develop their language proficiency and increase their intercultural awareness. The author provides engaging examples of ways to use this tool, as does the third case study, in which Blyth describes the development of an open source annotation tool called eComma, which turns reading into a group activity by encouraging learners to help each other understand a text. eComma provides readers with guidance and feedback during the reading process and allows learners to analyze texts in a collaborative and exploratory manner.

2.2.   Sharing resources

The second section includes three examples that illustrate the benefits and challenges of sharing and reusing resources. First, Motzo describes the contribution made by learners in the creation of reusable and adaptable digital and interactive materials. She argues that the creative engagement of the learners leads to an increase in both their participation in the learning experience as well as their appreciation of the importance of gaining transferable skills.

Conversely, Winchester focuses on her own experience as a teacher engaged in the practice of repurposing resources, and provides practical advice on how to select and adapt OER based on different pedagogical criteria. She reflects on the process of reusing and adapting resources for language teaching, and how this process can contribute to the professional development of teachers.

Calvi, Motzo and Silipo close this section with a description of a collaborative experience of producing audio-visual OER to help Italian learners with the pronunciation of specific sounds. They report on the advantages of working and sharing openly, and reflect on the benefits that working collaboratively can have for individuals and institutions.

2.3.   Sharing practice

The four case studies in the third section focus on sharing practice amongst teachers in the context of projects that harness openness to maximise the impact of professional development activities. First, Watson describes the experience of a group of part-time language teachers involved in the FAVOR (Find a Voice through Open Resources) Project, aimed at spreading the word on the advantages of open working and sharing amongst part-time teachers. Through the use of interview data, the author investigates the impact of the teachers' involvement in the project on their professional practices. She concludes that the most significant outcome of the project may have been the teachers' increased awareness of the learning design inherent in their own OER and those of other people.

A similar experience is described by Borthwick and Dickens with reference to the Community Café project. Through it, a community of open practice amongst community-based language teachers who were new to OER and OEP was fostered by providing a space to create and publish open educational resources related to their teaching. The authors provide practical examples of teacher involvement, and discuss some of the issues that should be considered when reaching out to a culturally diverse community group. They conclude that working with OER and OEP can impact significantly on the professional lives of community-based language teachers as long as participants are given the necessary time to absorb the new knowledge effectively.

Another initiative is presented by King, who describes the Onstream Project, aimed at encouraging collaboration and the sharing of resources and pedagogical approaches between teachers of Russian in supplementary schools, who are often volunteers working in isolation, and those in a mainstream secondary school and a university's Russian Department. The collaboration involved an online discussion forum, a resource bank for sharing materials and lesson observation. The researchers found a number of obstacles in the development of a culture of sharing among teachers, including contextual differences in the production and use of the materials, the variety of pedagogical approaches and, significantly, psycho-sociological factors inherent to the act of sharing with strangers.

Finally, Duensing, Gallardo and Heiser look at the collaborative development of OER from a staff development perspective. They present a project that aimed to promote open practices in a blended teaching context through collaborative writing and peer review of resources. They describe the various steps and activities in the project and discuss the gains in understanding of social online tools, and the enhancement in teaching practice that can result from teachers collaborating openly in the creation of OER.

2.4.   Collaborative learning
and student-generated content

The fourth section in this publication comprises a selection of case-studies dealing with student-generated content and collaborative learning. Rossade opens this section with an interesting example of the use of task forums to promote open discussion amongst learners in an advanced German course. He looks at the learning benefits of engaging in open communication in a protected environment, and the potential of using the resulting learner-generated content as a teaching resource in itself. Iglesias Mora and Leeming take this one step further by involving some of their beginners' Spanish learners in turning the content generated through forum discussions into open educational resources. They present examples of how the forum activities can be turned into open resources, and discuss the benefits for learners deriving from their engagement in this process.

Another two interesting case studies explore different ways of utilising materials made available openly through the OpenLIVES project (Learning Insights from the Voices of Émigrés from Spain). Nelson and Pozo-Gutiérrez present the collaborative work undertaken at the University of Southampton, which involved a group of undergraduate students in the production of learning materials based on the oral histories gathered by one of the authors in the course of her research into immigration. The authors discuss how the process was central to students' language learning but also provided relevant academic knowledge of cultural and historical events. In addition, the learners developed a range of very relevant skills such as transcribing and subtitling. Martínez-Arboleda uses the same resources as the basis for a final year module in which his students learn to become responsible digital scholars gaining a critical and ethical understanding of the social, epistemological and educational issues of economic migrations in Spain in the last century.

This section closes with Goria's description of the open course Collaborative Italian (Collit), an online learning initiative which targets adult students of Italian and provides them with a communicative language learning experience based on collaboration and social interaction. Through the use of a wiki, it requires learners to take responsibility for their own learning outcomes by repurposing open online resources to create new learning materials to be shared within the learning community. The author reflects on the difficulties caused by high dropout rates and varying levels of proficiency, although she found that the learners who participated in Collit showed increased engagement and involvement with the learning process.

## 2.5.	Learner autonomy

The last section in this book comprises two studies on learner autonomy. First, Capellini explores how creating OER can enhance student autonomy in the context of a self-study environment. He argues that, in order to benefit fully from the potential offered by OER, learners need to be aware of and open to different ways of using them. He also claims that learner autonomy does not imply learning alone, and that the mediation of teacher and peers is a necessary condition for the experience to be successful.

In the last case study, Beaven discusses the possibilities offered by MOOCs to supplement English for Academic Purposes courses at university level, and shows how they can enhance the learning experience by providing on the one hand content that is academically more relevant to the individual's studies, and on the other a higher level of choice for the learner to use the resources that are more appropriate to their language needs and personal learning style. The effect on learner autonomy will potentially be beneficial in terms of the individual's lifelong learning process.

## 3.	Final words

We hope that this wide-ranging selection of case studies will provide practical and inspiring examples of how OER and OEP can become part of the language classroom, to be used by both teacher trainers and practitioners in different educational contexts. Our ultimate aim, however, is to showcase the fact that there is no one way to engage in "open" practices in language teaching, and that there are multiple ways of pursuing "openness" in language teaching. Ultimately however, there is one constant which emerges from all of these case studies: the belief that engaging in open practices not only benefits students and their learning but also teachers by providing access to new tools, ideas, and communities from all around the world.

It has been a pleasure for us, as editors, to work together (albeit while being in three different countries and timezones) on this project over the past year. We are delighted to help make public through this book the important work that our colleagues are doing in the area of OER, OEP and language instruction around the world. We hope that you will find these case studies as inspiring as we did.

References

Downes, S. (2011). *Open Educational Resources: A definition*. Retrieved from http://www.downes.ca/archive/11/07_18_news_OLDaily.htm

ICDE. (2011). *International Conference on Data Engineering*. Retrieved from http://www.icde2011.org/

Pantò, E., & Comas-Quinn, A. (2013). The challenge of open education. *Journal of e-Learning and Knowledge Society, 9*(1), 11-22. Retrieved from http://www.je-lks.org/ojs/index.php?journal=Je-LKS_EN&page=article&op=view&path%5B%5D=798

Open Tools
for Collaboration

1 Communicating Out in the Open: The WordPress Class Blogs Plug-In Suite and Language Learning

Barbara Sawhill[1]

Abstract

This case study discusses the development of the Class Blogs Plug-In Suite in WordPress in order to create a blogging tool for use with all levels of language classes. The template, which is openly accessible and independent of a Learning Management System (LMS), creates an open, online learning environment that not only provides students with the ability to post their own work as well as comment on their classmates' work, it also has the potential to transcend individual classroom conversations and allow conversation to happen with language speakers around the world. This template was developed over the past 10 years, with the help of language teachers and students, and with the aim of facilitating the class blogging experience: it creates a central page that aggregates information from students' individual blog posts, images and videos in one central location, making it much easier to connect and comment with classmates. The template also provides easily accessible information on number of words blogged, number of posts written as well as number of comments made on others' blogs as a way to encourage language production and a sense of community. Concurrent with the exploration of the blogging template, this case study will provide suggestions on how teachers can encourage connections with the outside world, and examples of how students have accomplished thoughtful, integrated learning in the open environment of a blog to further their language learning.

Keywords: blogging, collaboration, WordPress, student-centric learning.

1. Oberlin College, Oberlin, OH, USA; barbara.sawhill@oberlin.edu

How to cite this chapter: Sawhill, B. (2013). Communicating Out in the Open: The WordPress Class Blogs Plug-In Suite and Language Learning. In A. Beaven, A. Comas-Quinn, & B. Sawhill (Eds), *Case Studies of Openness in the Language Classroom* (pp. 11-22). © Research-publishing.net.

1. Context

Educational blogging is not a new phenomenon. Over the past decade several free blogging tools have been created for educators to use with their classes. In addition, many learning management systems (e.g. Blackboard, Moodle, Sakai) now incorporate blogs into their standard set-ups.

There are shortcomings with these versions of blogging tools, however. Quite often there is a "one-size-fits-all" feel, and users reported that they felt limited by the ways in which they could configure the technology to suit personal preferences or to address the students' specific learning outcomes. Teachers have reported informally that older blogging tools forced them to change their teaching to fit the tool instead of using a tool that reinforced their teaching methodologies.

Many blogging tools presume that teachers and students want to work within a closed environment where the students in a class could only read and write posts with their classmates. As our teachers began to weigh the pros and cons of open versus closed, many began to question whether a closed blog was any different from a discussion board.

In addition, teachers began to ponder the kind of learning that might happen if their language students' writing and commenting was open to the world. Was there a way to balance the possibilities of open-ness with security and privacy concerns? Would native speakers read students' posts and leave comments? And if so, what would they say and how would the students react?

Teachers are not always technologists, nor do teachers always work in schools that have staff that are willing to customize a blog to meet a faculty member's needs. As a result, many teachers can become frustrated and disenchanted with the generic blogging tools, and choose not to use them at all.

The Class Blogs Plug-In Suite is a combination of multiple plugins and a single theme for use with WordPress, an open-source blogging and publishing platform. The source code for the tool is open and available to be downloaded, shared and adapted as needed. The goal of the Class Blogs Plug-In Suite is to make WordPress easier for students and professors to use when blogging as a class, an activity that the Cooper International Learning Center has been encouraging and supporting since the spring of 2007. While in 2007 we received only modest initial curiosity that semester, with two small classes experimenting with blogging, we soon saw curiosity turn into much more sustained interest in class blogging, with an average of seven classes blogging per semester, generating approximately 100 posts per class, with class sizes ranging from as few as 10 to as many as 60 students.

Regardless of whether teachers choose to use the Class Blogs Plug-In Suite, this case study will discuss both a rationale and a strategy for using open blogging in the language classroom as a way to increase student engagement with authentic language and culture via the web.

2.　　Intended outcomes

The intended outcomes were to develop a tool that:

- was scalable (class sizes ranged from 10 to 60 students);

- would work in all of the eight languages taught;

- was easily customizable (i.e. able to incorporate multimedia, to activate templates and plugins to suit personal preferences, etc.);

- could provide teachers with an efficient way to track and access content created by students;

- would strike a balance between a student's individual blogging space as well as a class blog aggregation tool.

The following pedagogical goals were also developed. In particular, it was decided that language teachers wanted:

- to explore effective ways in which teachers could connect their students with native speakers using technology;

- to encourage students to take (calculated) risks in a second language by writing about topics of personal interest and receiving feedback;

- to discover blogs and bloggers in languages other than English and in places other than the United States.

3.   Nuts and bolts

Most of the technical terms used in this case study will be familiar to those with experience in WordPress. However, there is a slight divergence between the standard terms used when talking about WordPress and the terms used in the following paragraphs. Specifically, WordPress refers to a setup where multiple sub-blogs are managed by a single primary blog as a multisite network, with each sub-blog designated as a site. This case study, however, refers to the primary site as the *parent blog*, and every other site as a *child blog*. With this exception, the rest of the terms used are in line with WordPress's standard terminology.

3.1.   Aggregation of posts

Figure 1 shows the front page of the parent blog, which is a template that aggregates all of the posts from the student (or child) blogs. Unlike most blogs where posts are arranged horizontally with the most recent post is at the top, this theme was created to organize students' posts in a more inclusive manner. Excerpts of the students' posts can be seen at the same time on the same page. Each time a student publishes an entry, his or her blog appears in the upper left hand corner of the page, nudging all of the other posts to the right and down, but not off of the front page.

Figure 1.   Front page of the parent blog
(http://languages.oberlin.edu/courses/2011/spring/hisp205/)

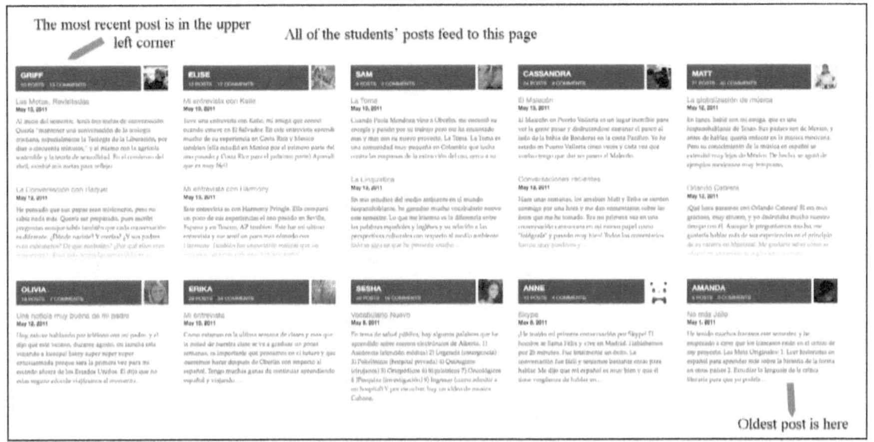

3.2.   Keeping track of content

Teachers expressed a desire to be able to get a sense of the students' production on an 'as needed' basis. As seen in Figure 2, the tool counts the total number of posts generated by the student as well as the total number of comments that student has made on other students' blogs within the class.

Figure 2.   Close up of the child blog as seen on the parent blog

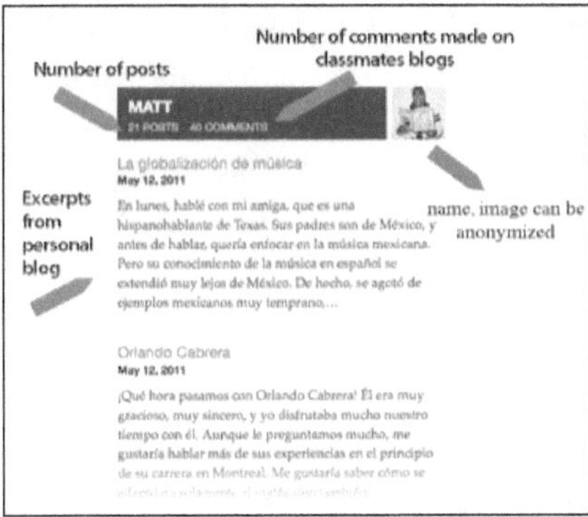

Another plugin was created to help keep track of the total number of words generated by each student throughout the semester (see Figure 3).

Figure 3.   Total number of words created by the student, per week

Week of	Adiel
Mar 18, 2013	601
Mar 25, 2013	588
Apr 1, 2013	1,401
Apr 8, 2013	349
Apr 15, 2013	753
Apr 22, 2013	443
Apr 29, 2013	446

3.3.   Protecting student identity

Teachers and students alike have grown more concerned about how their personal information might be accessed online. Educational institutions also worry about privacy issues when classwork is created and shared in open spaces. As a way to address these concerns, the tool allows students to blog under a different name (visible in Figure 2).

3.4.   Multimedia

Students are encouraged to incorporate images and YouTube videos in their posts, but in past iterations of the blogging tool it was difficult to find them. A plugin was created for the parent blog sidebar, allowing all images and YouTube videos that were posted elsewhere to appear in the sidebar, with a link back to the blog of origin.

4.   In practice

In order to take full advantage of the language learning that can happen via open blogging, teachers need to understand the ethos of blogging. Successful blogging depends upon reciprocity; it is not enough to post one's thoughts and wait for comments. Instead, bloggers need to seek out and comment upon the work of other bloggers, as a way to build community, but to also bring readers back to their blogs.

Given that there are, on average, two blogs created every second, it is statistically unlikely that a students' blog will be noticed and commented upon unless an effort is made to connect with bloggers outside of the classroom.

How does one find bloggers in other languages and countries? One way is to search for blogs via a list of the regional Google domains (list of country-specific domains).

To access the advanced blog search in any Google domain, follow these two steps (see Figure 4). The steps are exactly the same in any language and any domain.

Figure 4.   Locating blogs in Google
via a specialized search

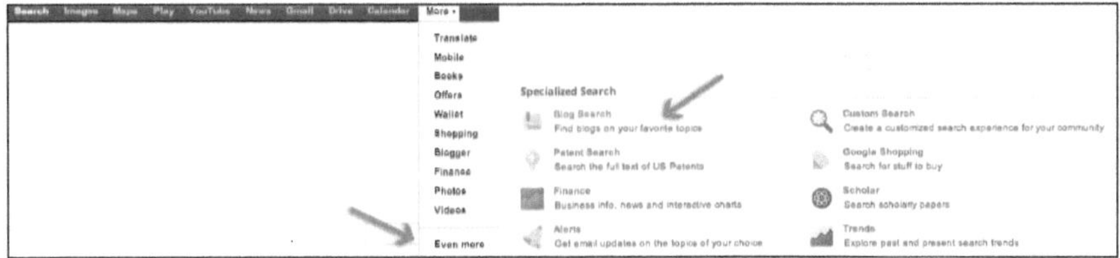

Students can search the blogs for topics, keywords, etc. of interest with the ultimate goal of reading and commenting on another blogger's posts in the target language, but also encouraging reciprocation from the blogger by leaving a url to the student's blog along with their comments.

Blogs in the language classroom are an excellent way for students to explore and converse about their personal interests in the target language. Examples of students using blogs in this way can be seen in Figure 5, Figure 6 and Figure 7.

Claire was interested in graffiti art in Latin America. After researching blogs written in Spanish about graffti, she encountered a blog created by women graffiti artists and began to leave comments and ask questions. To her delight, the artists started leaving comments on her blog posts as well. Over time the conversations moved from the asynchronous format of the blog to a synchronous instant messaging tool (as seen in Figure 5).

Figure 5.   Claire interacting with women graffiti artists /bloggers

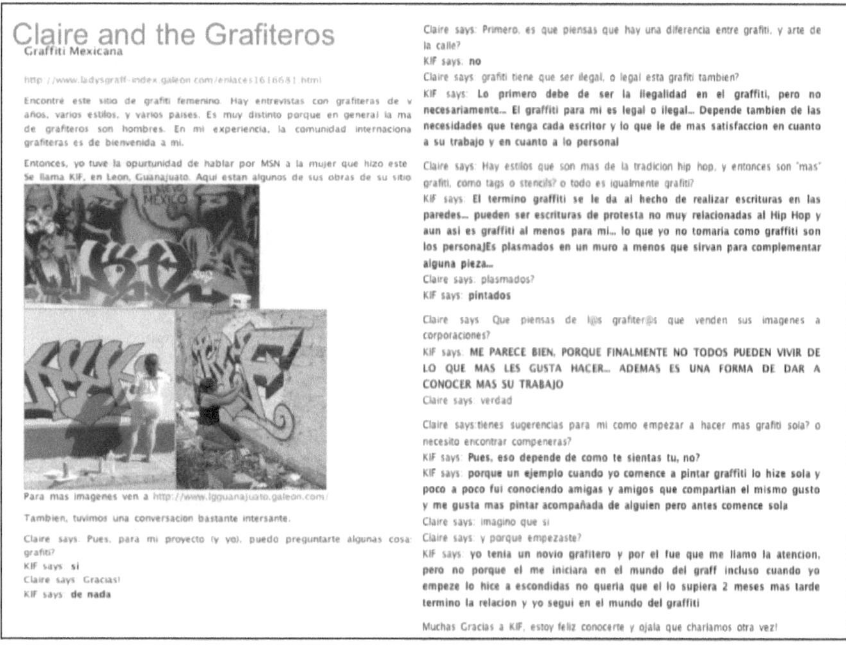

Evie used her blog to write about her experiences when studying in Ciudad Juárez, México, and to share information about the femicides that were happening at an alarming rate during her stay. She used her blog to connect with contacts she had made in México and to discuss ongoing efforts to solve the tragedy of so many women being killed at that time.

At the end of the semester, Evie received an unsolicited comment from the mother of Brenda Lerma Pineda, a 17 year old woman who had been found brutally murdered in México (as seen in Figure 6). The mother sent her letter in the comment section of Evie's blog with the instructions that it be sent "to the congress of your state" in order that the perpetrators "be punished in accordance with the severity of their crime".

For Evie, this was a remarkable moment. The horrible reality of femicides was no longer something she was blogging about from a distance. One of the families affected was now contacting her via the blog and asking for support in their quest for proper punishment for their child's murderers.

Figure 6.   Evie and the Mexican femicides

LOS COMENTARIOS

Eva de casa amiga, Te escribo esta carta para que insistamos ante la camara de diputados sobre la reforma al articulo 18 constitucional para que los delitos graves cometidos por los menores de edad , sean castigados de acuerdo a su gravedad. soy Mamá de Brenda Lerma Pineda, les redacto una carta esperando la hagan llegar al congreso de su estado y a todos los congresos de los estados de la republica. espero su contestación, comentarios y respuesta, mil gracias atentamente Miguelina pineda de Lerma.

nuevamente gracias por su espasio.

CARTA ABIERTA PARA TI.

QUE LA MUERTE DE MI HIJA NO QUEDE IMPUNE.

Han pasado 9 meses del asesinato de mi hija BRENDA LERMA PINEDA. Una chica de 17 años, sana, tranquila, buena niña, estudiante de preparatoria, con muchas ilusiones y planes para su vida futura. El dia 21 de octubre mi hija, fue encontrada muerta, acuchillada, violada, degollada y con mas de 40 puñaladas, le arrebataron su vida sin piedad y de la forma más cruel y sanguinaria.

El 11 de noviembre del 2005 se capturaron 3 de los asesinos, y dan por finalizada la investigación. Sus declaraciones son diferentes de cada uno de ellos. En la reconstrucción de hechos no mencionaron los dos orificios de aguja hipodérmica que se encontraron en el ante brazo de mi hija. (el cuerpo fue encontrado cerca del pueblo en un cañaveral)

Sean was a passionate student of music composition and theory. He also expressed a growing interest in the art of teaching and in the process of learning. Sean was able to mesh all of his worlds and his passions – Pedagogy and Spanish and Music – into his class blog (Figure 7). Thinking of the hours he had spent teaching himself in anticipation of his Conservatory studies, Sean created a blog that was a guide, a syllabus, and a tool to help others learn as well. As a result his Spanish 305 blog was an openly available study tool for Spanish speakers interested in Music Theory and Composition. He wrote about the process of blogging as follows:

> I quickly found that blogging was a good way for me to show – myself – that I knew what I was talking about. It demanded that I understood my material and actively thought about it and the clarity with which I was teaching. I also had to weigh countless movements, works, and names from over a century of music literature against one another, and then I quickly found that while I could avoid bias, I still tended to write most clearly about what I understood best – AND what I was more passionate about.

Figure 7.   Sean's blog

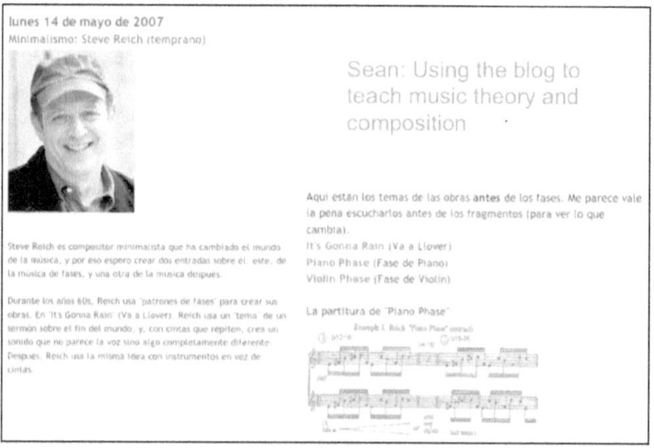

Towards the end of the semester, he received this comment:

> Hola!!!!! buscando datos sobre impresionismo llegué a tu información. La verdad que esta muy bueno como explicas los movimientos, me intereso

> sobre todo el Impresionismo porque tengo que dar unas clases prácticas en secundario y estoy buscando información para que a los chicos les resulte didáctico, entretenido y puedan aprenderlo... [sic]

In this comment the writer, a secondary school teacher in Argentina, was looking for information about how to teach Impressionism to her students. She found Sean's blog and asked for his guidance in teaching the subject to her students. Through their interactions on the blog, Sean's writing became a valued resource for the teacher and for her students. Sean commented:

> Short and sweet, the blogging system to me demonstrated that I am not the ignorant Spanish student I thought I was, and helped instill the first thoughts of pedagogy into my mind – I have been thinking about education differently ever since.

The remarkable connections that Claire, Evie and Sean experienced via their blogs happened because they were invested in their subjects and were eager to share and learn out in the open, and because the tool they were using made their work available to the outside world.

5.   Conclusion

The Cooper International Learning Center at Oberlin College has worked with faculty to create an open source blogging tool with built-in plugins that allow faculty and students to engage in conversations with their classmates, and with people beyond the classroom. The blogging tool was customized to allow faculty better and more efficient access to the work being done by their students, as well as allowing students an easier way to add multimedia, tags, comments and text about topics that were of interest to them.

When used as a place for students to explore and write about personal areas of interest in the target language, blogs can provide a space outside of the closed learning management system to explore ideas and potentially connect with others. Those connections may need to be cultivated intentionally, but when they do happen, blogs can provide an excellent opportunity for students to engage with authentic language practices and to learn about culture first hand.

The Class Blogs Plug-In Suite was developed and tested in WordPress version 3.3. It has been downloaded over 3,000 times from the WordPress plug in site. As is the case with other OER, it is available for others to adapt and improve and then share back with the community. We welcome the community's participation in its continued development as well as feedback about the extraordinary connections that can happen through this tool.

Acknowledgments. The author wishes to acknowledge the work of Justin Locsei for the development of the Class Blogs Plug-In Suite, as well as the students in HISP 205 and 305 at Oberlin College for the work they have done using these blogs over the past ten years. In particular, she would like to thank Claire Miller, Evie Levine, and Sean Hanson for their dedication to their projects and for sharing their work with others.

Useful resources

A list of the courses (language and non language) that have used this tool: http://languages.oberlin.edu/cilc/blogs/archives/

A list of international Google domains: http://en.wikipedia.org/wiki/List_of_Google_domains

Further information about blogging and language learning: http://languagelabunleashed.org/series/teaching-transparently/

The Class Blogs Plug-In Suite: http://wordpress.org/extend/plugins/class-blogs/

Wordpress: http://wordpress.com

2 The Mixxer: Connecting Students with Native Speakers via Skype

Todd Bryant[1]

Abstract

The Mixxer was created at Dickinson College in Pennsylvania, USA as a way to connect language students with native speakers as part of a mutual language exchange. The site began as a potential solution for one instructor who had difficulty finding a reliable class-to-class partnership for her Japanese course and has since grown to include over 100,000 users representing more than 100 languages and is used by a number of academic and government institutions around the world. Built using Drupal and integrated with Skype, the site allows for individuals and instructors to connect in a variety of ways including individual exchanges between language learners, class to class exchanges, and events. Events are invitations organized by an instructor inviting potential language partners to sign up to speak with their students at a given day and time. For writing practice, the site provides a blog function allowing learners to post and ask the community for feedback. For instructors who would like to keep track of language exchanges completed by their students as homework, there is also a confirmation function. The student can send their partner a form asking that they confirm the exchange after which a summary then appears on their confirmation page.

Keywords: eTandem, Skype, CMC, language exchange, social network, open tools.

1. Dickinson College, Carlisle, Pennsylvania, US; bryantt@dickinson.edu

How to cite this chapter: Bryant, T. (2013). The Mixxer: Connecting Students with Native Speakers via Skype. In A. Beaven, A. Comas-Quinn, & B. Sawhill (Eds), *Case Studies of Openness in the Language Classroom* (pp. 23-31). © Research-publishing.net.

1.   Context

Dickinson College is a small liberal arts college located in a rural part of the United States. Like many institutions, Dickinson wanted to connect students studying a second language with native speakers interested in improving their English skills, an invaluable cultural as well as linguistic experience.

About ten years ago, one of the first goals for using technology in the languages was to take advantage of new chat clients with added voice capability. Exchanges via text chat at Dickinson were already somewhat established, including a class in the French department which did regular exchanges with a high school in France. A teacher in the Japanese department became interested in doing the same for Japanese, though she required that the exchange be verbal, since the beginning and intermediate students would not be able to type at a speed that would make text chatting feasible.

Finding and maintaining a synchronous voice exchange with a class in Japan proved very difficult. However, after several weeks of leaving posts on forums, writing to various listservs, and trying to leverage institutional partnerships abroad, a teacher of English interested in an exchange was eventually found. The exchanges were still very time-consuming to organize, due to different expectations from each side, academic calendars, and the thirteen-hour time difference.

The Mixxer, as seen in Figure 1, was originally envisioned as a way for teachers to find each other and connect for class-to-class exchanges. Potential teachers could provide information about the type of exchanges they were seeking, available times, and technical capabilities in order that a more productive partnership could be found. While creating the site, the decision was also made to allow individual learners to sign up, although there was no foreseen use for these accounts at the time. As the site grew, however, this pool of independent language learners allowed us to schedule "events", an invitation to users sent via email using their profile information from the site to contact Dickinson students, at a given time via Skype.

Figure 1.   The Mixxer homepage

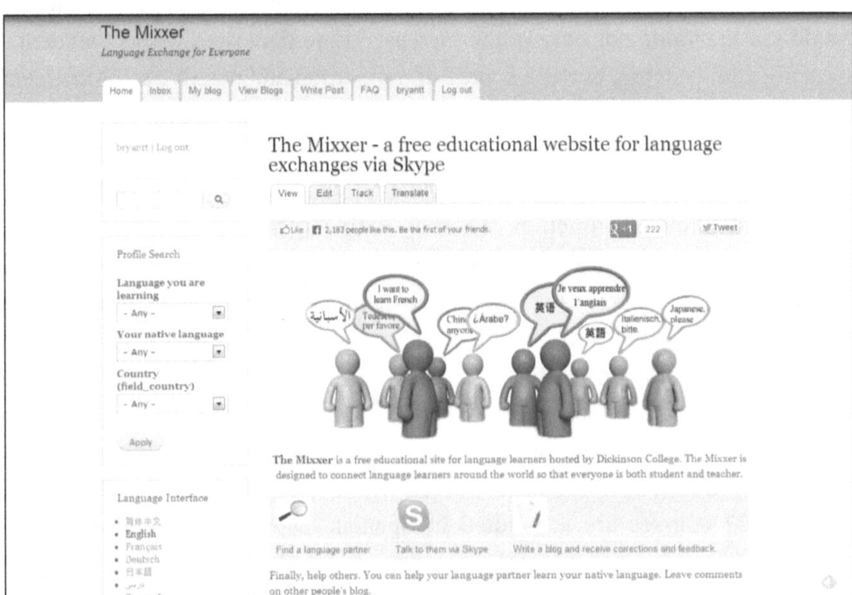

Using the Mixxer, it became possible to provide exchanges to almost any class, regardless of language and time with only a few days' notice from the teacher.

2.   Intended outcomes

When creating the Mixxer, there were two principal goals. The first was to make the process for organizing these interactions as easy and flexible as possible. By doing so, student verbal competence was expected to improve along with an increase in authentic cultural interactions.

In 2006 there had already been many studies that demonstrated the benefits of synchronous computer mediated communication, although at the time they had focused almost entirely on text chats.The expectation of the project was that by creating a system that allowed for the ability to organize verbal exchanges for

Dickinson students on short notice, and with a format flexible enough to support conversations by students from the beginning to intermediate levels, teachers would see the value not only in the increased time dedicated to each student's speaking and listening, but as a source of motivation and positive reinforcement as well.

The steady increase in new users to the site, currently roughly 100 per day, and a system "event" function, whereby native speakers are invited to sign up to speak with Dickinson students one on one, allows any teacher on the site, whether from Dickinson or another institution, to organize an exchange for their students with only 3 to 4 days' notice. This is true for any foreign language at virtually any time of day. As a result, there has been a steady rise in the number of teachers who have added language exchanges as a regular part of the course at Dickinson College. In 2004, there were one or two courses in French and Japanese which interacted with native speakers. For the spring of 2013, 22 courses are scheduled in Spanish, Japanese, French, German, Arabic and Russian and several more are expected before the beginning of the semester.

The exchanges have proven to be popular with students as well. In the fall of 2008, teachers added four questions to the course evaluations about the exchanges via Skype. Roughly 90% of the students from the five Spanish courses, two Italian courses and one German course enjoyed the exchanges and thought they were beneficial to their language learning. A survey of Japanese students in 2007 demonstrated similar results with students giving an average rating of 4.9 on a scale of one to six from strongly disagree to strongly agree on questions about their enjoyment and perceived effectiveness of the exchanges.

3. Nuts and bolts

The Mixxer began and still is almost exclusively an individual project, although faculty from a number of departments use the system and have at times requested a feature. The most important example being the request from a Japanese teacher to build the "event" function, which has since been modified to make it easier for any teacher on the site to more easily organize events and have learners seamlessly connect via Skype.

Because a single person develops the site in addition to organizing most of the exchanges, it was important to find a system that made development as easy as possible, could scale to a large number of users, and would be free for the college. The original site was created from scratch using Microsoft's .NET framework; however, the project moved to Drupal when it became clear that a significant amount of programming effort would be saved by changing platforms and using Drupal's modules to add social networking functions such as messaging, contacts, and blogs. Instead of having to write extensive code for each of these functions as is done with .NET, Drupal already has modules that only need to be configured and occasionally modified with a few lines of php. Drupal has also become increasingly popular in education, and they've released distributions with modules already installed for many common uses in education including department websites, digital humanities, and courses.

4.   In practice

There are three principal ways that instructors use the Mixxer web site to connect their students with native speakers. The most common is to have the students register on their own, find a partner using the search function as seen in Figure 2, and complete the exchanges as homework. It's best to instruct students to have a topic and questions before the exchange. This is especially true for beginner and low-intermediate students. Because this does involve coordinating times with a stranger, one should be as flexible as possible concerning due dates. By assigning a certain number of exchanges per month or semester instead of per week, students with some planning can still complete the assignment even if their first partner has technical difficulties or is otherwise unreliable. Even if a student has difficulty connecting with their first partner, native English speakers should never have any difficulty finding another partner rather quickly with whom they can exchange on a regular basis.

Figure 2.   An individual search in the Mixxer

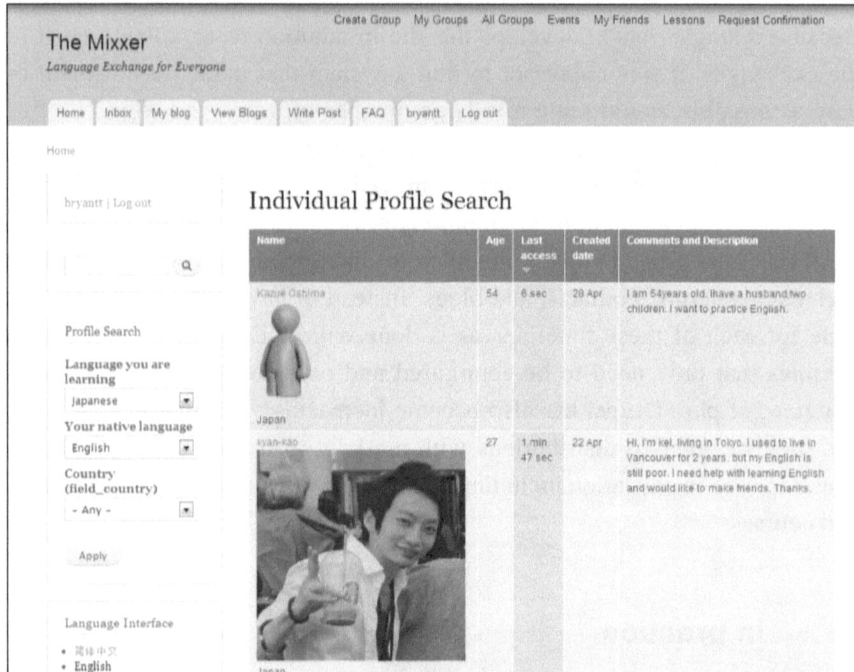

At Dickinson College, the most frequently used function to connect students is by using the "events". For the event, either the technologist or a teacher at the college announce the day and time on the website. Users who match the language profile then receive an invitation with a link where they can sign up. The instructor who organized the event can then see a list of users who signed up along with contact information as seen in Figure 3. On the day of the event, students meet in the computer lab. A text chat is sent via Skype to all of the native speakers who had signed up to take attendance. These Skype names are distributed among students who then initiate the call. For instructors interested in how the events work, a video is available on YouTube.

Figure 3.   Scheduling an event in the Mixxer

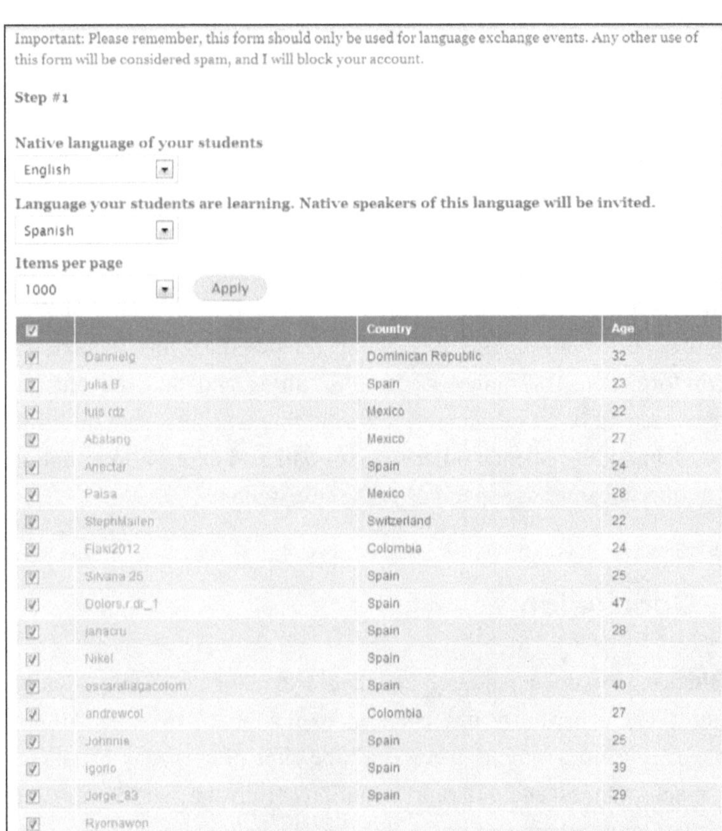

The disadvantage of the event format is that class time is required. The major benefit is that every student is able to connect every time, making for a more positive experience for the students as well as the teacher. Because there is a pool of individual users already connected on Skype, it is possible to match those connected with Dickinson students one-to-one using any extras to create group calls of three people. It is also less stressful for the students knowing their teacher is available for help. For this reason even if a teacher plans to assign exchanges outside of class, it is recommended to have one in-class event in order for students to gain some confidence and at least one contact. This function is available to any user on the site with teacher permission. Any professional educator is welcome to create an account on the site and then email bryantt@ dickinson.edu to gain this additional access along with more detailed instructions.

The final and original method for connecting students is the class search. This function is also only available to teachers and allows them to search for partner classes. As mentioned earlier, differing schedules, expectations and technical capabilities can make class to class partnerships very challenging. When successful, however, the benefits can make the additional planning time worthwhile, allowing students to develop relationships and work together on long-term projects. To minimize the difficulties and take advantage of the positive aspects of these exchanges, it is vital that teachers from both sides have a clear understanding of each other's class goals and expectations, and that they clearly communicate these specifics with their students.

5.   Conclusion

When thinking of open resources available to educators, one usually thinks of content. There certainly has been an explosion of excellent digital items available to educators ranging from YouTube clips of everyday language to high quality maps, images and 3D representations from the world's top museums. Indeed, they have become so numerous that the principal challenge has shifted from the creation of these individual resources to the creation and development of multiple interlinked databases that allow these resources to be found and presented in useful ways for teaching and research. However as more language instructors focus on communication, the ability to connect easily and reliably, asynchronously or in real time, and via text or audio is the most important advance in web-based technology over the past ten years. Students certainly benefit from the increased exposure to one-on-one communication with a native speaker linguistically, but it is at least as important as a way of providing students with an immediate practical use for their study and as a personal introduction to a culture with which they will hopefully engage for the rest of their lives.

Acknowledgements. Special to thanks to Akiko Meguro, Japanese instructor at Dickinson College, for her initial involvement in the project and suggesting the "event" function that was eventually added to the Mixxer for teachers of all languages.

Useful links

Drupal: https://drupal.org/node/1237536

The Mixxer: http://www.language-exchanges.org

Video of creating a Mixxer event: http://www.youtube.com/watch?v=XwM2_sktNSo

3 eComma: An Open Source Tool for Collaborative L2 Reading

Carl Blyth[1]

Abstract

Reading has increasingly become a social activity thanks to the rise of e-readers such as iPads and Kindles. This means that people can now carry on Internet-mediated conversations with others about the texts they are reading. This case study describes eComma, an open source web application for textual annotation developed by the Center for Open Educational Resources and Language Learning (COERLL). eComma turns reading into a group activity during which learners help each other understand a text. For example, readers mark up a digital text with tags and comments to which other readers may respond. Tags and comments are automatically displayed as word clouds for further analysis. Social reading tools such as eComma provide readers with valuable guidance and feedback during the reading process and thus allow learners to analyze a text together in a more collaborative and exploratory manner. Originally conceived as a tool to facilitate close-reading activities in the English literature classroom, this case study recounts how second language teachers are exploring eComma's potential. It is shown that eComma helps language learners' deal more effectively with unknown vocabulary and grammar. In addition, eComma's hypermedia environment heightens language learners' awareness of the process of textual interpretation.

Keywords: annotation, close reading, collaborative learning, multiple literacies, social reading.

1. University of Texas at Austin, US; cblyth@mail.utexas.edu

How to cite this chapter: Blyth, C. (2013). eComma: An Open Source Tool for Collaborative L2 Reading. In A. Beaven, A. Comas-Quinn, & B. Sawhill (Eds), *Case Studies of Openness in the Language Classroom* (pp. 32-42). © Research-publishing.net.

1. Context: Reading literary texts in a foreign language

Foreign-language learners frequently complain that reading literary texts can be a frustrating experience, mainly because of the hours spent hunting for definitions in the dictionary. And yet, there is great benefit to be gained from reading 'real' texts, rather than pedagogically 'doctored' texts so prevalent in the beginning stages of language study. Teachers sometimes attempt to solve this problem by providing lessons on reading strategies, especially the merits of contextual guessing. Teachers also try to lighten the reading load by glossing texts for learners. For example, LitGloss, an open access project from the University of Buffalo, provides digital versions of many foreign language short stories and poems that include grammatical and cultural glosses. Unfortunately, glosses are no panacea. In fact, glosses can actually make learners more passive and less apt to struggle with the demands of reading.

In 2009, a new tool called eComma was created to help struggling learners overcome the problems associated with the close reading of literary texts. Designed by faculty and graduate students from the Department of English at the University of Texas at Austin, the tool's main purpose was to enable a group of readers to build a commentary on a text and to search, display, and share the commentary online in a more pliable form than had previously been available. The tool was the result of a grant from the National Endowment for the Humanities, an independent agency of the US federal government and one of the largest funders of humanities projects in the United States. The tool was also partially funded by an internal grant from the University of Texas at Austin. In concrete terms, eComma provided a suite of free annotation tools and an online space for learners to read in a collaborative fashion.

Originally conceived to facilitate close-reading activities in the English literature classroom, the tool was soon adapted to the second language classroom. After all, reading foreign language texts – literary or non-literary – requires a close, word-by-word approach to textual interpretation. In essence, eComma allowed learners to 'crowd source' their reading burdens by turning a solitary activity into a group activity. In addition to relieving learners' frustrations over unknown vocabulary and grammar, eComma's hypermedia environment heightened learners' awareness of the process of textual interpretation.

The new tool gave rise to new pedagogical practices by turning reading into a social activity where different readers made different kinds of contributions to meaning-making teams. Some readers enjoyed looking up words in the dictionary. Other readers preferred tackling grammatical problems. And the teacher would often personalize the activity even further by assigning readers different roles to play in the process of interpreting a text. For example, the English literature teacher often began the lesson by handing each learner a note card on which was written a rhetorical device. Next, the learner quickly scanned the text on the computer and highlighted examples of the rhetorical device. After approximately ten minutes, the class had thoroughly marked up the poem with annotations for such tropes as *simile, synecdoche* and *metonymy*. After several more passes through the text, the learners were finally allowed to "read" the text in its entirety and to share their interpretations with each other. The result was an online, interpretive activity in which all learners seemed to be deeply engaged. In sum, social reading and collaborative annotation tools helped learners who were struggling with the demands of difficult readings by allowing them to become members of a team. Traditional approaches to reading force learners to perform the same task, that is, to read the text alone. In contrast, social reading allows learners to negotiate strategies for "dividing and conquering the text" with their classmates.

2. Intended outcomes: An open source tool for social reading

A year later, the developers of eComma granted COERLL (Center for Open Educational Resources and Language Learning) permission to reprogram the software in Drupal, a popular open source content management system. COERLL is one of 15 national foreign language resource centers funded by the U.S. Department of Education's Title VI Program whose mission is to produce and disseminate materials and best practices for language learning. The goal was to create a free, open-source version of eComma for any language at any level. Usability testing and pilot testing in foreign language classrooms took place from 2010-2011 at the University of Texas at Austin and at Cornell University. Based on these tests, COERLL undertook a complete redesign of the original eComma application. In addition to redesigning the interface, programmers at COERLL sought to assure that the new version of eComma would interact seamlessly with different browsers and different operating systems. Finally, another important goal of the redesign was to facilitate research on social reading. This was accomplished by allowing administrators and teachers to download the learners' tags and comments as an XML file. The XML file could then be imported to a Google Doc for analysis.

## 3.	**Nuts and bolts**

As a Drupal module, the new version of eComma is free and open to the public; however, it requires a server that runs Drupal. Similar to learning management systems such as Blackboard, content management systems like Drupal require technical support. Therefore, instructors interested in using eComma must first contact their computer support staff to determine whether Drupal is available on their campus. All necessary technical information about the eComma module can be found on eComma's Developer page. Directions on how to set up classes and upload texts can be found on the eComma technical page. eComma's system requirements for OSX 10.6 are Safari 5, Firefox 10 and Chrome 17 or higher. For Windows 7 computers, Firefox 10 or higher is required. Today, the open-source version of eComma has a brand new look and several new functionalities:

- a website with information about pedagogical applications of social reading;

- an extensive help page for users;

- a new set of icons to enhance navigation;

- an easy way to download comments and display them as an XML file;

- a simple way to import all user data to a Google docs spreadsheet for analysis.

4.   In practice

Even though the open-source version of eComma has been available to the public for only a short time, the new website already features several classroom case studies based on early pilot testing (Figure 1).

Figure 1.   eComma web site

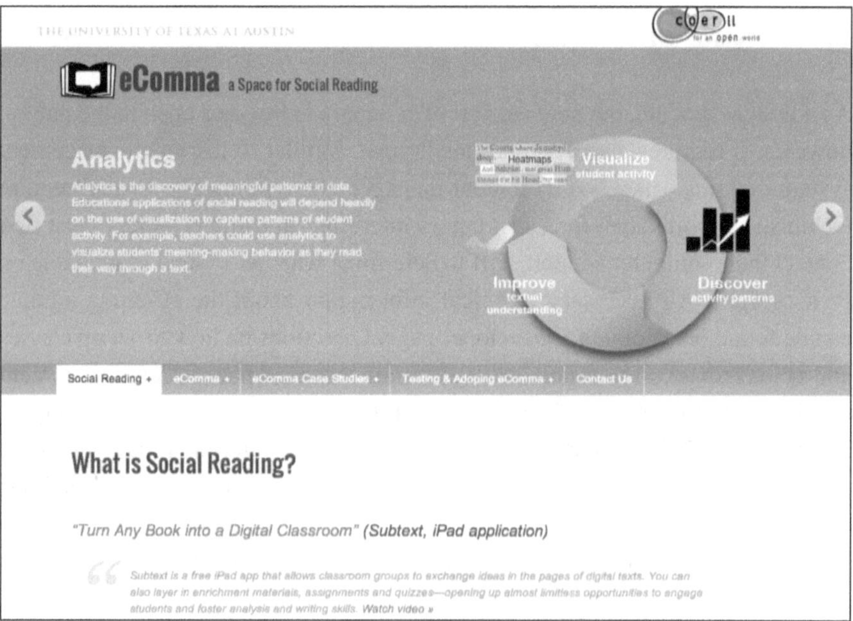

The first case study was based on a graduate course on linguistic variation in French-speaking societies at the University of Texas at Austin. For this activity, the teacher had the learners read a text written in Louisiana Creole, a short story titled *"L'espoir"*. Since there is no standard way to write Louisiana Creole, the author invented his own spellings, borrowing heavily from French orthography. The teacher told the learners to annotate as many variable spellings as they could find. To help them with the task, the teacher demonstrated how to use *eComma*'s word cloud feature to compare spellings (Figure 2). A word cloud is an alphabetical display of all the words that occur in a text in terms of their frequency – the more frequent the word in the text, the bigger the word in the cloud.

Figure 2.   Word cloud in eComma

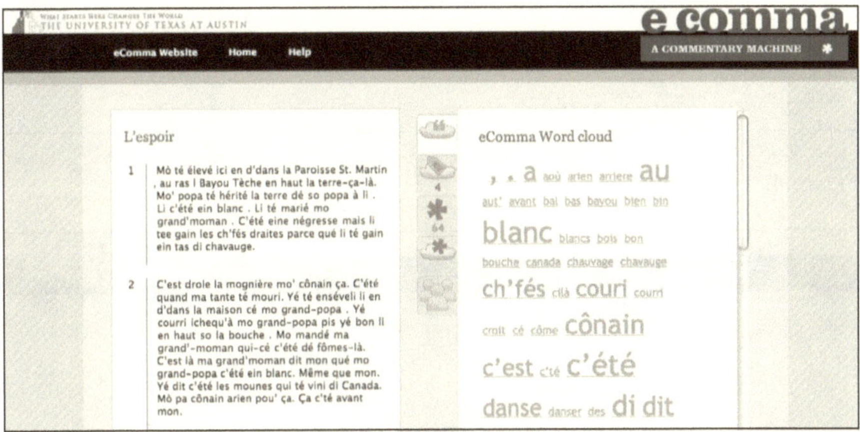

Several eComma features were useful for guiding in-class discussion. The teacher employed the heat maps to draw learners' attention to heavily annotated passages (Figure 3). This led to a discussion about the distribution of different forms of variation found in different parts of the text.

The teacher also used the user list feature to display the comments of individual users (Figure 4). This feature allowed the teacher to demonstrate that some learners paid more attention to nominal morphology and other learners were drawn to verbal morphology. Again, this insight became fodder for further discussion about learning styles and individual differences indexed by the learners' patterns of annotations.

Figure 3.   Heat map

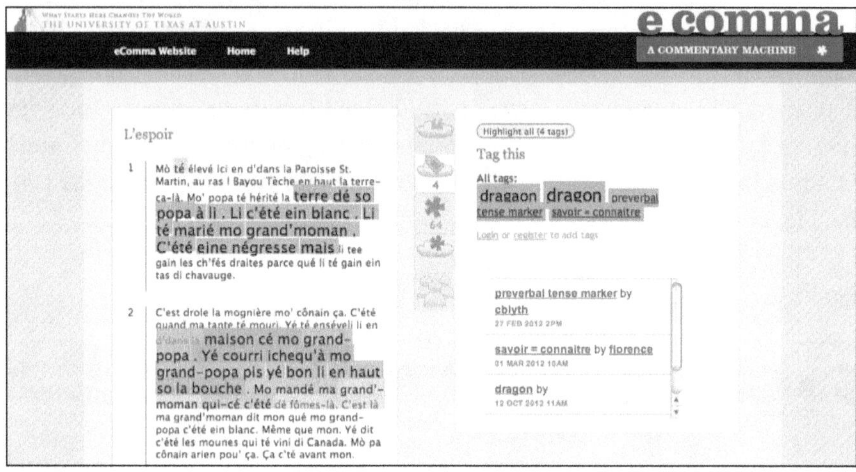

Figure 4.   User list

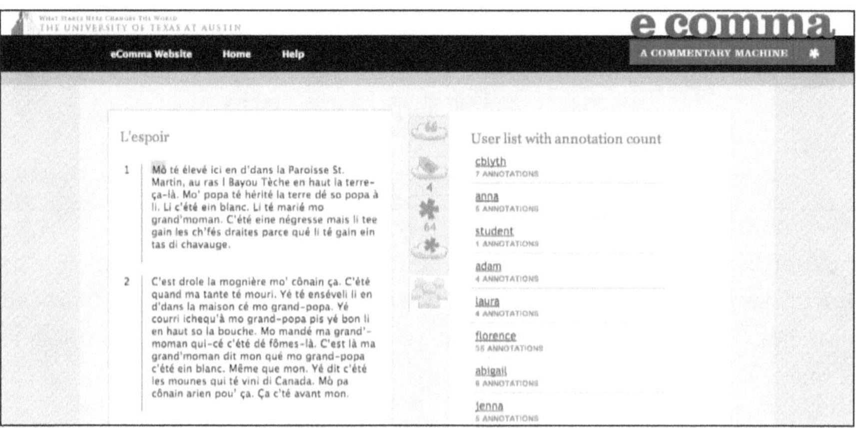

This case study of eComma demonstrates a consciousness-raising activity that is often used in second language classrooms to help learners discover form-meaning pairings. A more common example of this type of form-focused activity would be to have learners annotate different past tense forms found in a narrative text, e.g. preterite vs. imperfect. Comparing the different highlighted verb forms in context would help learners to develop their own hypotheses about the meanings of the narrative past tenses. The same could be done for other formal categories: singular vs. plural, definite vs. indefinite, active vs. passive, indicative vs. subjunctive.

The second case study came from its use in a fourth semester French course at the University of Texas at Austin. The teacher instructed the learners to annotate the poem "*Liberté*" by Paul Eluard (1942) in either English or French as part of their homework assignment, an example of an asynchronous use of the tool. The learners were to comment on how the surrealist poem's non-sequiturs and odd juxtapositions made them feel. The teacher was pleased to discover that learners often replied to each other's comments, evidence that they were reading each other in addition to reading the text. And finally, a few of the learners did something unexpected but very much in keeping with the surrealist text – they annotated the text with visual images taken from surrealist paintings! It was an excellent use of multimodal glosses that extended the previous day's discussion of the interaction between literature and the visual arts.

The third case study described how a teacher of beginner French at Cornell University devised a mid-semester reading activity that incorporated eComma. To supplement the textbook, the teacher compiled a selection of prose poems from Dany Laferrière's (1994) *Chronique de la dérive douce*, a book that recounts the first year that Laferrière spent in Canada as a refugee from the Duvalier regime in Haiti. As homework, the teacher had her learners read one of the poems online and share their exploratory commentaries on eComma in English. She followed this activity with a worksheet to assess her learners' comprehension. Based on her eComma "experiment", the teacher drew some preliminary conclusions about social reading:

- it precludes the need for certain kinds of pre-reading activities, especially those that forestall the productive process of grappling with meaning-making;

- it models effective reading strategies for learners who may not employ them on a regular basis;

- the inductive nature of social reading (discovering meaning through social interaction) heightens appreciation of the text and of the fruitfulness of collaboration.

The fourth case study was based on a graduate level course titled *Literacy through Literature* taught by a teacher of German at the University of Arizona. The course explored the role that literary texts and aesthetic reading played in the development of second language literacies. Literacy was used in the course both in the traditional sense of the reading of printed texts and in the wider sense of multiliteracies, which include social and cultural literacies as well as new media literacies. One of the readings for the course was a chapter from narratologist Marie-Laure Ryan's (2001) book *Narrative as Virtual Reality* on immersivity and interactivity as two modes of reading narrative texts. At the end of this chapter, Ryan introduces an example from the book *If on a Winter's Night a Traveler* by Italo Calvino (1979). The teacher decided to implement eComma in a synchronous activity that allowed her learners to consider Ryan's distinction between immersive and interactive reading, and to examine what kinds of pedagogical interventions might encourage one or the other mode of engagement. Here is how the teacher described what happened:

> "After the first few learners had created annotations, I noticed that almost everything that had been posted was an experiential response. I added a couple of comments of my own, including one about Calvino's use of the second person. I was curious to see if learners would follow my lead or if they would continue to post about their personal reading experiences. A couple of people did respond to my comment... [These comments] yielded productive material for our in-class discussion of the degree to which a text encourages either immersive or interactive readings. While [one learner] attempted to build upon what I had said by identifying

other familiar literacy practices in which the second person was used, the better portion of the annotations pertained to their personal reading experiences. Many of these related to the particular experience of working with eComma."

The teacher reported that while some learners experienced initial difficulty learning to annotate the text (she hadn't given the learners an introduction to the software since she felt it was so transparent), all agreed that the software held potential for working with texts in an L2 context. They appeared to be most excited about the flexibility of the software. Several noted that the program could also be used as a space to share learners' findings during a text-anchored Internet research activity.

5.   Conclusion

OERs (Open Educational Resources) represent a heterogeneous group of materials that fall on a continuum of size and complexity – from the large-scale OERs such as online courses produced by well-funded institutions to the small-scale OERs such as a set of lesson plans produced by a single instructor. eComma constitutes a large and technically complex OER. It has been funded by two grants from federal agencies of the U.S. government – the National Endowment for the Humanities and the National Foreign Language Resource Centers. In addition, the development of eComma has been made possible by the resources of a large research university that has played a key role as an incubator for the pedagogical application of collaborative annotation.

When COERLL began development of eComma several years ago, social reading was in its infancy and most annotation software was proprietary. Today, thanks to the popularity of e-readers, social reading is on the rise. As a consequence, more annotation tools have become publicly available. And yet, these tools are largely limited to specific platforms, including eComma. What is needed is an interoperable tool that will plug into a school's learning management system or

LMS, that is, the software application used by an educational institution for the delivery of online courses (e.g. Blackboard, Canvas, Moodle).

Unfortunately, the current version of eComma is programmed in Drupal 6 that is quickly being superseded by Drupal 7. By sharing eComma's source code, COERLL hopes to lower development costs and to increase collaboration among interested parties. As one of the fastest growing open source content management platforms, Drupal has a large and active community of developers, many of whom work at universities and colleges. Regardless of eComma's future, COERLL aims to create a community of practice around *open annotation tools* that will bring together teachers, learners, researchers and developers interested in exploring the pedagogical affordances of social forms of digital reading.

Useful links

Center for Open Educational Resources and Language Learning (COERLL) http://www.coerll.utexas.edu/

Drupal https://drupal.org/

eComma Developer Page http://ecomma.coerll.utexas.edu/ecomma-developer-page/

eComma Technical Page https://drupal.org/sandbox/coerll/1782670

eComma Website http://ecomma.coerll.utexas.edu/

LitGloss http://litgloss.buffalo.edu/litgloss/about-litgloss.shtml

National Endowment for the Humanities http://www.neh.gov/

University of Texas at Austin https://www.utexas.edu/

References

Calvino, I. (1979). *If on a Winter's Night A Traveler*. San Diego: Harcourt Brace.

Eluard, P. (1942). *Poésie et Vérité*. Paris: Éditions de Minuit.

Laferrière, D. (1994). *Chronique de la dérive douce*. Montréal: Les Éditions du Boréal.

Ryan, M-L. (2001). *Narrative as Virtual Reality*. Baltimore: The Johns Hopkins University Press.

Section 2.

Sharing Resources

4 The Linkedup Project:
An Online Repository for Language Teachers

Anna Motzo[1]

Abstract

LinkedUp is a repository of open educational resources (OER) aimed at language teachers and learners between 4-19 years. The main aim of the project was to tackle the shortage of free high quality online materials. The author examines how the use of technology and a 'learner-centred' approach led to the creation of engaging new learning activities. During the creative process, emphasis was placed on collaboration and openness with participants encouraged to share ideas throughout the project. This case study focuses on one project whose aim was to combine language learning with business studies and illustrates how learners, through a mixture of formal and informal activities and settings, contributed to the creation of the learning materials. It reports on how this creative engagement led to an increase in both the learners' participation in the learning experience and in their appreciation of the importance of gaining transferable skills. At the end of the project a collection of reusable and adaptable digital and interactive materials was added to the site. This case study is part of a growing body of research on how the OER movement is democratising learning. However, as many of these projects still rely on short-term external funding, concerns are expressed about whether OER repositories are sustainable in the long term.

Keywords: Italian, language learning and teaching, learner-centred approach, open educational resources, technology.

---

1. The Open University, London, UK; A.Motzo@open.ac.uk

How to cite this chapter: Motzo, A. (2013). The Linkedup Project: An Online Repository for Language Teachers. In A. Beaven, A. Comas-Quinn, & B. Sawhill (Eds), *Case Studies of Openness in the Language Classroom* (pp. 45-56). © Research-publishing.net.

1. Context

The *LinkedUp Award Scheme* ran between 2009 and 2011 and was aimed at producing innovative and creative teaching materials for language teachers in primary, secondary and post-16 settings. It was the product of a fruitful collaboration between various UK based language associations and led by the Association for Language Learning (ALL).

The Association for Language Learning is an association for teachers of foreign languages at all levels which provides professional development activities and is responsible for a series of language learning and teaching publications. ALL led the LinkedUp scheme together with Links into Languages: a language specialist consortium led by the Subject Centre for Languages, Linguistics and Area Studies based at the University of Southampton (which specialises in educational projects and professional development for language teachers) and the Specialist Schools and Academies Trust, a non-for-profit organisation which aims to raise learner achievement levels in schools in England and internationally.

The main principle of the award scheme was 'learning through sharing' and participants were encouraged to share ideas and work together in the creation of an online repository specifically designed for language teachers. The platform was also viewed as a staff development opportunity since the development of new teaching approaches and ideas were an integral part of the projects.

The scheme encouraged collaboration between different institutions and contributions from different areas of expertise. It funded four types of collaborative projects that encompassed ten different themes which reflected national priorities in language learning, such as the need to address aspects of the national curriculum which most required further development. The types of funded projects included partnerships coordinated by a school, a 16-19 college, a local education authority, a teacher training provider or a university language department.

The project themes included re-engaging hard to reach pupils in language learning; supporting and recognising pupils' home languages and/or plurilingual approaches to language learning; developing pupils' linguistic independence and confidence in speaking; encouraging employer engagement in language learning (supported by CILT, the National Centre for Languages); building languages into work-related learning for 14-19 year olds and creating a smooth pathway of progression between key stages. By August 2011, the scheme had managed to fund 112 projects across the UK.

This case study focuses on a LinkedUp funded project entitled 'The Language of Business', led by the author in the academic year 2009-2010 while working as Italian lecturer and language coordinator at City of Westminster College (CWC), an inner-London Further Education College. In order to widen learner range of professional competence and future employability in a global business environment, CWC offered a variety of vocational courses including work based National Vocational Qualification (NVQ) awards in languages (in French, Italian and Spanish) at levels 1 and 2 (equivalent to beginners or A1-A2 Common European Framework), to post-16 learners enrolled in a Business and Technology Educational Council (BTEC) National Diploma in Business, which is a vocational qualification rated at level 3 on the National Qualification Framework. However, as the NVQ Languages units were not formally integrated into the Diploma in the Business course, learners consistently undervalued the language component and its relevance leading to repeatedly low rates of attainment.

In collaboration with the business teaching team, it was decided to run a pilot course of Integrated BTEC Diploma in Business with Italian and the author produced a new syllabus and new interactive online learning material. It was in this context that the LinkedUp project management team were approached.

2.   Intended outcomes

The main purpose of the pilot was to enhance learners' motivation and language skills by increasing their engagement in language learning. The experiment focused on only one language – Italian – as it was the most at risk within the College.

The project priorities were identified as the need to rethink the way languages were delivered and the crucial importance of learners obtaining realistic out-of-classroom language experience designed to develop both their language and business awareness and competence. Five specific outcomes were set:

- to offer an alternative language delivery model for languages at CWC in business diploma courses;

- to increase learners engagement in language learning;

- to improve linguistic progression and motivation;

- to promote integration of language and business by working closely with professionals who use languages in their day to day jobs;

- to produce a new cutting-edge, online learning resource pack specifically tailored to NVQ Italian language students enrolled on a business Diploma course.

In order to achieve the above mentioned outcomes, a new scheme of work, which integrated NVQ Italian into the Business units, was written and new teaching and learning resources specifically based on interactive, authentic and innovative material were devised. Specific task-based activities for the learners were set by the author in collaboration with the business studies representatives and supervised by the business studies coordinator in order to ensure that the tasks fitted with the curriculum.

The crucial innovation of the pilot was that learners, through the *in situ* element, were helped to develop a wide range of appropriate technical business vocabulary and linguistic structures suitable to their levels. The pilot also encouraged students to sharpen their business communication skills by setting specific tasks which involved: following employers' instructions, carrying out market research, making formal presentations, writing reports and taking part in a focus group.

All the briefs and tasks were filmed and subsequently new interactive learning activities were created and eventually added to the LinkedUp repository for other teachers to use, adapt and modify. One further aim was to help develop the interest and awareness of students who were not directly involved in the project.

By doing so, 'The Language of Business' project addressed the two main aims of the LinkedUp award scheme:

- to address national priorities in language learning;

- to tackle the shortage of good online materials by producing a bank of innovative and creative new resources which are freely available to teachers and learners.

3.   Nuts and bolts: 'The Language of Business' project in detail

The pilot was organised in accordance with the parameters set by LinkedUp. Specifically, the author was appointed project leader and worked mainly with three business organisations:

- Lavazza, the Italian coffee maker;

- Giacobazzi, an Italian deli shop based in Hampstead, North London;

- I-mage, an Italian PR and Marketing organisation based in London.

The project leader's main duties were to liaise with the other project partners, coordinate schedules of activities, maintain regular contact with the LinkedUp management team, produce a report at the end of each phase of the project and eventually write and produce the new teaching material for the repository. In order to guarantee efficiency, all partners and learners had to agree in advance the schedule of work and three meetings (one for each project phase) were organised with each business. The pilot consisted of three phases:

- **preparation**: a period of 6 weeks of detailed planning;

- **implementation**: a period of 3 months during which the project was carried out with a group of 10 students;

- **resources development**: a period of 2 months in which the resources were produced and the materials eventually disseminated.

Initially, a shared *Google* workspace was set up for partners to communicate and share documents, although emails and telephone calls remained the most used forms of communication. Secondly, an action plan was devised to both set the agenda for visits and meetings and set deadlines for the completion of activities.

During the first phase the main representatives planned a set of activities and tasks for students to carry out during the second phase. The team capitalised on each business' particular area of expertise and the activities were planned in such a way that, by completing each task, students would provide evidence of having achieved specific language and business based outcomes.

Specific business areas which would provide the context for the activities were selected:

- Marketing;
- PR;
- Customer Care;
- Market Research;
- Investigating business.

Whereas the focus in the language component was on the:

- development of specific/technical vocabulary;

- development of basic language structures;

- acquisition of basic grammar.

During the second phase, the project involved:

- visits to the business partners;

- producing videos and audio recordings featuring both businesses and students;

- hosting a lecture on Marketing by one of the business partners.

Finally, during the third phase the learning material was produced using videos, *PowerPoint* presentations and *Word* documents. All the resources were tested in the college first and were uploaded in the college's *Moodle* platform so that students could work on the material both in the classroom and independently. Students were also encouraged to use this platform to work collaboratively in the development of wikis to improve Italian business vocabulary.

4.   In practice: A practical example of the type of resources produced

'The Language of Business' project was designed to be learner-centred, fun and innovative. All the language learning workshops were run face-to-face and they were carried out both in the classroom (formal learning), and out-of the classroom in a business environment (informal learning). The language approach used in both formal and informal settings was communicative and based on the 'chunks theory' as it was thought that this would suit beginners best (Krishnamurthy, 2002). Nevertheless, they occasionally had to deal with quite complex language structures and vocabulary. This approach was reflected in the production phase of the resources. These focused on:

- giving a business presentation;

- giving a demonstration;

- following instructions.

All the material produced, in accordance with the LinkedUp scheme's directives, was divided into the following sessions:

- general files: documents providing an overview of the specific project;

- resources for pupils: main learning material pack which included activity aims and objectives, stimuli (audio/visual format) and activity templates;

- further resources for pupils: testimonials, feedback, students sample of work;

- resources from the partner school.

4.1.   Structure of the activities

Each set of activities has clear language and business objectives (Figure 1 and Figure 2).

Each set of activities starts with a *stimulus*. In this example (see Figure 3), a video interview with the Marketing team of Lavazza UK was produced, followed by the creation of learning activities which were used both interactively via an interactive whiteboard and as a printed worksheet[1].

---

1. See 'Lavazza filmed interview in Italian', http://www.linksintolanguages.ac.uk/resources/2354.

Figure 1.   The front page of the Lavazza Case-study

Figure 2.   The unit's objectives

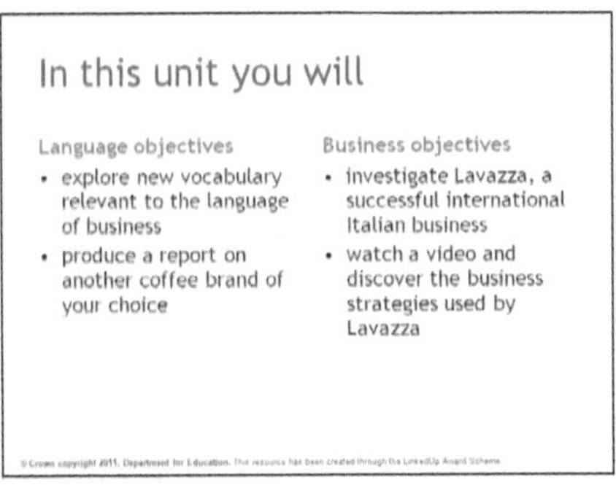

Figure 3.   The video interview

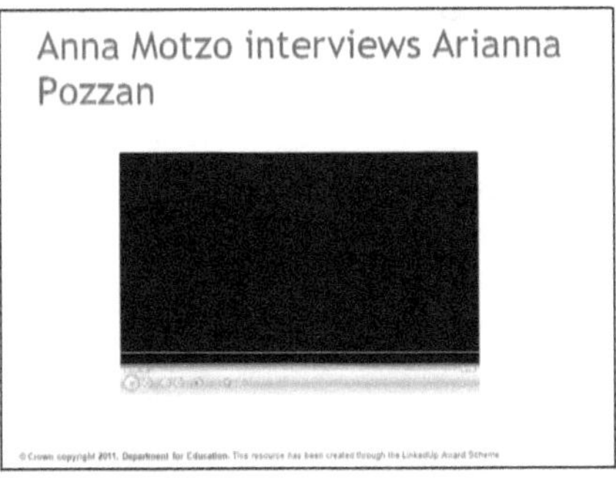

Figure 4. First learning activity

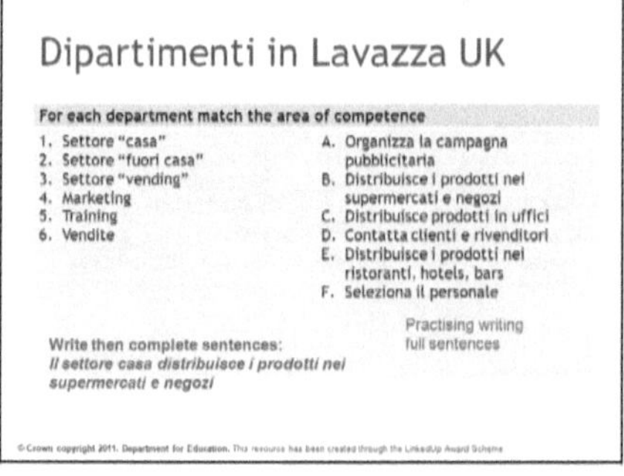

Figure 5. Second learning activity

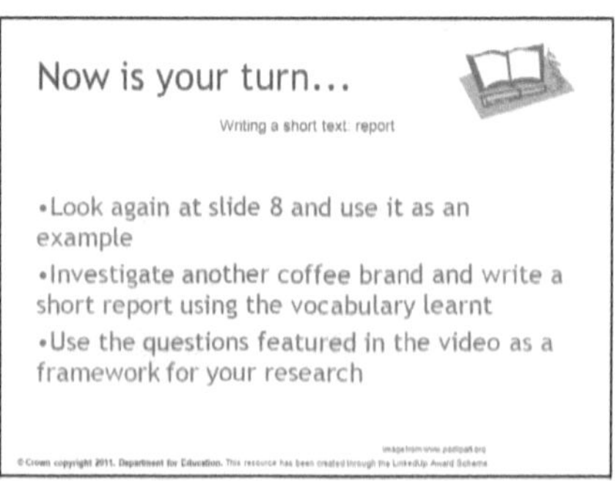

Figure 6. Third learning activity

Then, learning activities (Figure 4, Figure 5 and Figure 6) were created and used both interactively via an interactive whiteboard and as a printed worksheet[1].

5.   Conclusion

As stated, the author's rationale for taking part in the LinkedUp award scheme was to develop more innovative and engaging materials which could be shared openly as an example of good open educational practice.

During the development of the project material, the principle of openness was applied by:

- opening up the context of language learning into out-of classroom activities;

- sharing ideas with fellow colleagues and the project management team on how best to meet the set outcomes. This aspect of the process was pivotal to keep standards high and to minimise production of less relevant resources;

- opening the language learning experience to the use of different tools and new media in order to make it more engaging for the learners.

Once tested, the resources produced were published under Crown copyright licensing, which allows users to reproduce the material for internal circulation, research and teaching or training purposes, provided that the material is acknowledged as Crown copyright. The material can also be adapted, provided that the original source is acknowledged.

The LinkedUp Scheme now contains a valuable repository of educational resources with a wide range of teaching materials. The dissemination of this

---

1. Ibid.

initiative has been very successful and it was unfortunate that the scheme was closed in 2011 due to government funding cuts and that there are no plans to curate and manage the resources beyond 2013.

Although it is conventional that government-funded projects of this kind have a short shelf life, it is to be hoped that some means will be found to allow the resources in the LinkedUp repository to find a new home, perhaps through some form of cross institutional collaboration.

Acknowledgements. Kathy Wicksteed, Programme Lead, LinkedUp Award Scheme; David Rogers, Marketing Director, Lavazza UK; Kingsford community school, project school partner, South East London, UK.

Reference

Krishnamurthy, R. (2002). Language as chunks, not words. *Jalt 2002 Conference Proceedings* (pp. 288-294). Retrieved from http://jalt-publications.org/archive/proceedings/2002/288. pdf

Useful links

Association for Language Learning: http://www.all-languages.org.uk
Centre for Languages, Linguistics & Area Studies: https://www.llas.ac.uk/
CILT, the National Centre for Languages: http://www.cilt.org.uk
Language of Business resources: http://www.linksintolanguages.ac.uk/resources/2354
Linkedup Project: http://www.linksintolanguages.ac.uk/linkedup/index.html
National Curriculum: https://www.gov.uk/national-curriculum/overview
Qualifications Frameworks: http://ofqual.gov.uk/qualifications-and-assessments/qualification-frameworks
Specialist Schools and Academies Trust: http://www.ssatuk.co.uk

5 Repurposing Open Educational Resources: Creating Resources for Use and Re-use

Susanne Winchester[1]

Abstract

This case study draws on work carried out as part of an Open University (OU) project on collaborative writing and peer review of open educational resources (OER). The article focuses on one teacher's experience of repurposing (i.e. re-using and adapting existing resources for different purposes) OER, examines how access to open repositories for OER can enhance teachers' own practice and reflection process and illustrates the processes involved in repurposing. Selecting suitable resources for repurposing can be based on image suitability, resource format, content suitability or on information gained from teacher's notes, descriptions or tags. It will also be demonstrated how resources can be designed for a particular teaching context and how resources can be made fit for re-use. The case study gives practical advice on how open images can be sourced and how using Creative Commons licences can assure that resources are shared in the way the author had intended. A checklist offers practitioners who are interested in using and designing OER guidance for the repurposing process.

Keywords: repurposing, reversioning, creative commons, task design, re-using, adapting, open educational resources, OER, teacher practice.

---

1. The Open University, UK; s.winchester@open.ac.uk

How to cite this chapter: Winchester, S. (2013). Repurposing Open Educational Resources: Creating Resources for Use and Re-use. In A. Beaven, A. Comas-Quinn, & B. Sawhill (Eds), *Case Studies of Openness in the Language Classroom* (pp. 57-69). © Research-publishing.net.

---

1.   Context

The case study was carried out as part of the general scholarship activity at the Open University (OU), UK, under the umbrella of 'Scholarship of and for Teaching'. It was one of 9 projects in 2011-12 and focused on the integration of the OU language repository LORO into the professional development of Associate Lecturers (here referred to as teachers) at the Department of Languages in the Faculty of Education and Language Studies.

LORO, the online repository used by the Department of Languages at the OU came into being through a JISC funded project in 2009/10 to develop a repository for storing, sharing and accessing language teaching resources and was launched in January 2010. LORO holds OER for language teaching provided by the Department of Languages, teachers and external users. Languages taught at the OU comprise Chinese, English for Academic Purposes, French, German, Italian, Spanish and Welsh. All language courses range from beginners to upper intermediate, apart from Chinese and Welsh which can only be studied at beginners' level, and Italian which can only be studied at beginners' and lower intermediate. The resources held are used by teachers in tutorials, which can either take place face-to-face or via the Elluminate programme. Elluminate is a web conferencing programme used for delivery of online, synchronous tutorials. Many of the resources on LORO are specifically designed for this particular environment.

The current initiative arose from the need for an opportunity for teachers to engage in the design process of OER in collaboration with colleagues, while experiencing the benefits of peer review within the LORO environment.

The aim of the project was two-fold: firstly, to improve the functionality of LORO and secondly, to organise a series of staff development events with a focus on collaborative design of open educational resources and peer reviews.

Twelve teachers (teaching English for Academic Purposes, French, German, Italian and Spanish at various levels) participated in the project, led by a project team involving seven course developers/coordinators and regional language coordinators.

Four groups were formed and over four meetings participants engaged in collaborative writing, either producing materials from scratch or, where a cross-curricular approach was taken, repurposing existing resources. The examples given in this article were created within the latter framework and aimed at beginners' level. Each group member produced resources, which were peer reviewed throughout the design process.

2. Intended outcomes: Understanding effective repurposing

The author was particularly interested in understanding how resources in the repository can be approached for repurposing. Her own particular aims for the activity were:

- exploring ways of searching for and selecting resources for repurposing;

- repurposing resources designed for use with interactive resources for online teaching;

- exploring how resources can be made fit for re-use.

In the following sections each of these aims are addressed in detail and some specific observations are outlined.

3. Nuts and bolts: Exploring ways of searching for and selecting resources for repurposing

Resources in LORO can be searched in a variety of ways: by course code, language, language level, author or tags (browse view). While it makes sense to search for activities at the same level, it is also useful to consider other levels. It is a great way to see colleagues' approaches to materials design. It aids one's own professional development and can encourage reflection.

Once materials were selected for consideration for adaptation or repurposing, it became obvious that a more systematic approach in selecting suitable resources needed to be taken. The following approaches emerged:

- selection based on **image suitability**;

- selection based on **resource format**;

- selection based on **content suitablilty**;

- selection based on information gained from **metadata** and **teacher's notes/lesson plans**.

3.1.   Suitability of images

Images are an ideal way of getting language learners to speak without having to resort to copious instructions and text. Therefore, the first search involved searching for images within resources and tasks that could either be used in the same way as in the original resource or could be reused in a different task design.

The advantage of using images from OER language resources in LORO is that a) they have already been selected on the grounds that they fit a language learning context, and b) many of them are used because they are copyright-free images or have sources acknowledged. However, this is not always the case and great care must be taken when selecting images for use and reuse.

Wikimedia commons is a good source of images. Here, images can be searched by categories and licensing information accompanies each image. Royalty-free images can also be found on Flickr commons and Google images but it is important to check any licensing attached to them by running an advanced search. In all cases, sources must be acknowledged. This applies also to any use of clip art, e.g. Microsoft or clip art from sites such as Open Clip Art Library.

3.2.   Resource format

A large part of the resources held on LORO are designed for use with a web-conferencing programme. The system allows teaching resources to be uploaded as PowerPoint presentations, image files (png) or whiteboard files (wbd) amongst other formats. The advantage of using whiteboard files is that, unlike PowerPoint or image files, whiteboard slides can be designed with moveable objects, such as text boxes or images, which can be manipulated by teacher and learners. The majority of resources officially designed by the Open University are in whiteboard format, while resources from OU teachers or outside contributors may come in a range of formats. Therefore, in order to increase interactivity and to fully exploit the affordances of the tool, only resources that had been originally created as a whiteboard file were considered.

3.3.   Content suitability

Browsing through a repository is more than just a search; it engages the practioner with examples of resources created by peers and can thus develop one's own practice and open up new ways of approaching a topic. Therefore, where a repository does not hold any resources whose constituent parts can be re-used, searching through the resources can nevertheless inspire new creations purely based on an idea. In a distance learning environment where meeting fellow teachers face-to-face is a rare occasion, having the opportunity to see colleagues' work and teaching methods can be beneficial and inspiring but also reassuring.

One of the huge benefits of LORO is the technical facility that allows posting feedback and comments (Figure 1). Not only is this useful feedback for the creator of the resource but it is also a useful indicator for those who are considering using the resource. In line with common practice elsewhere, resources can also be 'liked'.

Figure 1.   Comments on a resource

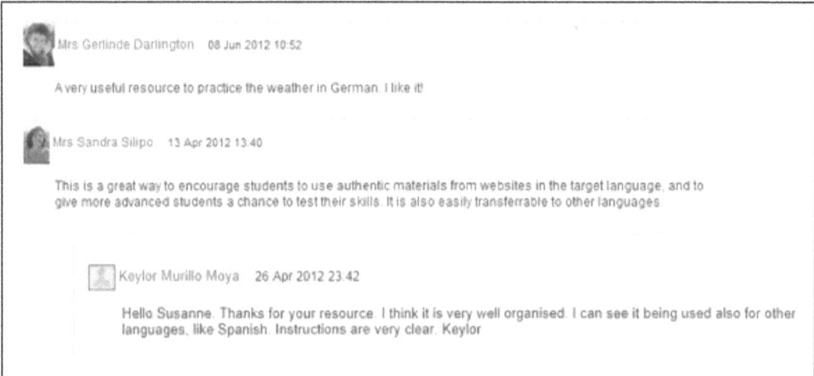

3.4.   Value of metadata
and teacher's notes

Many resources (especially those produced by the OU) include teachers' notes or lesson plans. These support documents are essential where materials themselves are not self-explanatory or where a resource was selected on the basis of its visual strength rather than language or level (e.g. by a teacher who is not proficient in the language). In those cases, any guidance relating to the teaching procedure is vital. In addition to teachers' notes which, if present, form part of the download package, metadata in the form of a description of the resource, tags, creator, permissions and download rate are all helpful criteria in the selection process (Figure 2). Tags are particularly important as these are searchable and therefore the more accurately they describe the resource, the more effective the search.

Having considered a variety of resources in LORO in this way, three resources were selected for repurposing.

Figure 2.   Metadata attached to a resource

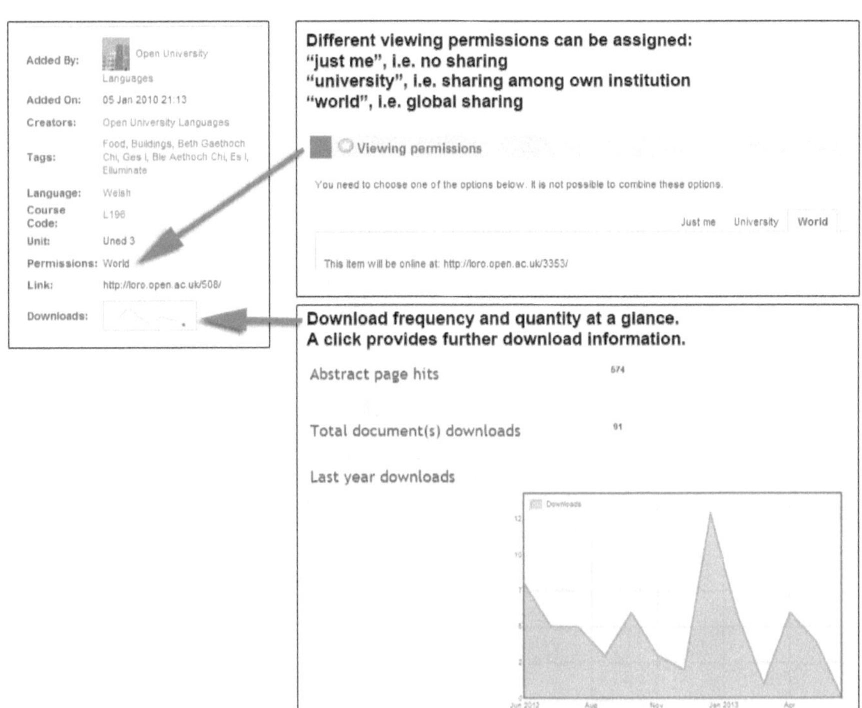

4.   In practice: Repurposing resources

In the following section some specific examples are presented of how the repurposing process was approached.

4.1.   Repurposing images

In the example below an Italian resource for practising directions was selected. This resource had already been reversioned from a Spanish resource (all resources mentioned here can be found in LORO).

Figure 3.   Original Italian resource for practising directions

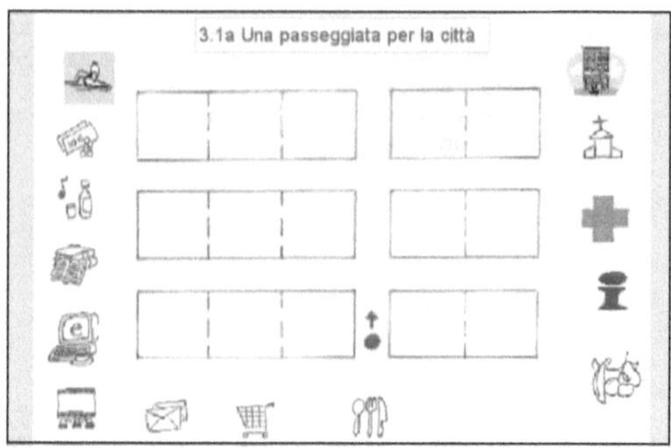

Figure 4.   German resource based on the Italian resource on directions

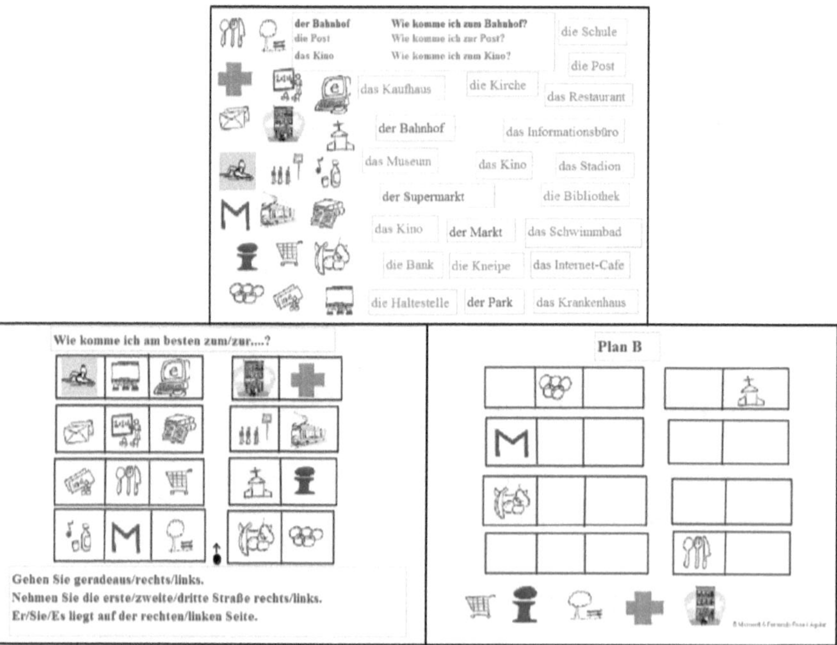

The selection decision was made on the basis of suitability of the visual content
of the activity. The resource contained very little taught language but was

completely relevant to German, so therefore the images could be used while the language could be adapted. The resource consisted of three different slides, including a map with moveable image tiles for learners to use in an activity on directions (Figure 3).

For the first stage of the activity only images representing places in town were used. The activity was adapted to deal with a) gender (colour coded vocabulary) and b) the case endings in the question 'Wie komme ich zum/zur...?' (How do I get to the...?). The second original slide was used but here slightly more language scaffolding was provided to compensate for the particular difficulty of case endings and use of subject pronouns in German. The last stage of the original activity was reused without much further adaptation (Figure 4).

4.2.   Repurposing content and ideas

In this example (Figure 5), the idea of using a weather map formed the basis of a weather resource. Here, too, further language scaffolding was provided for learners to make maximum use of the visual as a speaking stimulus. By including the web address the source was acknowledged but it also enabled future updating for anyone who wanted to repurpose this activity.

Figure 5.   Original and reversioned weather activity

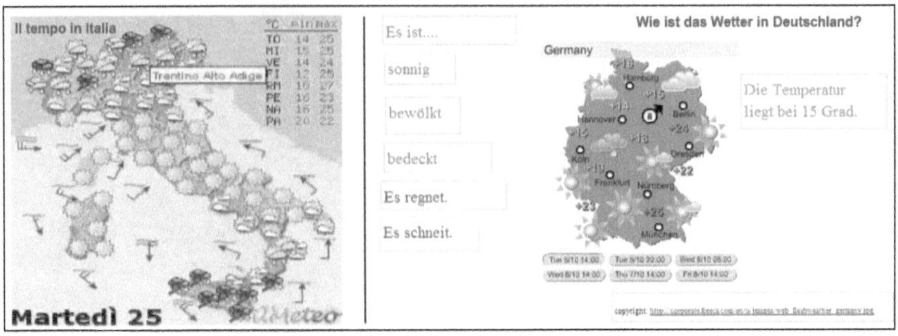

The next section of the original resource inspired another similar activity but one which incorporated a web search (Figure 6).

Figure 6.   Original and reversioned table for weather activity

Le previsioni del tempo

Data: 5 aprile

Città	Temp.min	Temp.mass	Previsioni
Milano	18	25	Nuvoloso
Venezia			
Aosta			
Bolzano			
Roma			
Campobasso			
Bari			
Olbia			
Palermo			

Der aktuelle Wetterbericht

Stadt	Tiefsttemperatur	Höchsttemperatur	Wie ist das Wetter im Moment?
Kiel			
Hamburg			
Bremen			
Hannover			
Düsseldorf			
Berlin			
Dresden			
Frankfurt			
Stuttgart			
München			

Gehen Sie auf diese Webseite:
http://wetter.spiegel.de/spiegel, und suchen Sie die Tiefsttemperatur, Höchsttemperatur und das aktuelle Wetter.

4.3.　　Repurposing led by metadata and teachers' notes

The third resource was selected on the basis of information gained from its metadata. Although the tags, containing phrases in Welsh, did not help, it was useful to have a description of the activity. As the images were clear and easy to re-use for an activity in German, the activity was divided into two parts, both, however, practising the past tense, just as in the original activity. In addition to the images, vocabulary was included to help with the decision whether to use the article or not when talking about what had been eaten and drunk the day before, using the Perfect tense (Figure 7).

Figure 7.   Original and reversioned activity to practise the past tense

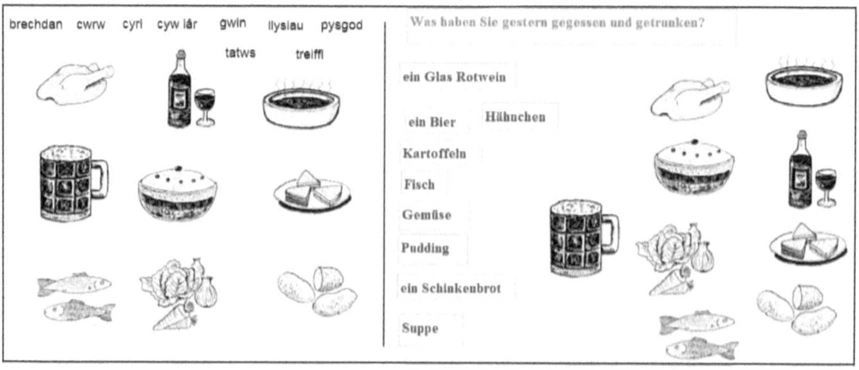

As the next original whiteboard slide contained practice for places in town with a preposition, the same could be replicated for German. Considering the stage of study and ability of learners, more language help was needed, so before launching into the main activity, a matching activity was designed because gender was important for knowing whether to use 'zum' (to the + masculine or neuter noun) or 'zur' (to the + feminine noun) (Figure 8).

Figure 8.   Original and reversioned activity

4.4.   Exploring how resources can be made fit for reuse

The project and resource design raised the question of whether resources should be created solely for one's own use, or whether any consideration should be given as to how the resource can be used beyond the creator's own purpose. If the resource is intended for maximum distribution, then it must be designed and 'packaged' appropriately so that it can be located, used and repurposed.

The following checklist aims to offer a practical approach to producing OER, which can easily be repurposed by others.

Packaging for repurposing - Checklist

- Are the images and other sources I use copyright free? Have I acknowledged all sources?

- Have I credited the original resource author?

- Is the resource format accessible by others? If not, how can I ensure that access is possible? (For example, if the repository has a preview function, ensure that files can be previewed) Can the resource be made available in other formats?

- Am I producing content that is sufficiently broad for it to be useful for others?

- Am I packaging my resource in such a way that I am providing sufficient information and metadata about it so that it can be found easily?

- With whom am I sharing my work? Sharing can either be purely on an institutional level or can be global. This will depend on the openness of the repository.

- How do I intend the resource to be used? How widely do I share my work and what do I allow users to do with my resource, i.e. how do I license my resource?

Creative Commons offers a range of licences that combine different aspects such as attribution, non-commercial use, no derivatives and share alike (derivative resources must be shared under the same license as the original). The Creative Commons Licenses page contains detailed information on all the available licenses.

5.   Conclusion

Having access to a repository consisting of colleagues' work offers an invaluable insight into ways of approaching the same subject and thus provides an opportunity for reflection, personal and professional development.

At the same time, sharing our own resources means that we can extend their life-cycle. By sharing resources we can also make a contribution to the wider teaching community. If we share in a way that makes it possible for everyone to access our resources, we can help support colleagues, while enhancing our own practice through feedback and reflection.

Useful links

Creative Commons http://creativecommons.org

Creative Commons (licenses) http://creativecommons.org/licenses/

Elluminate http://en.wikipedia.org/wiki/Elluminate_Live

Flickr commons http://www.flickr.com/commons

Google images https://www.google.co.uk/imghp?hl=en&tab=wi

Italian resource http://loro.open.ac.uk/110

LORO http://loro.open.ac.uk/

LORO (browse view) http://loro.open.ac.uk/view/

Open Clip Art Library http://openclipart.org/browse

Spanish resource http://loro.open.ac.uk/3201

Wikimedia commons (images) http://commons.wikimedia.org/wiki/Category:Images

6 Designing OERs to Teach Italian Pronunciation in an Open Educational Environment: A Case Study

Anna Calvi[1], Anna Motzo[2] and Sandra Silipo[3]

Abstract

This case study reports on work that was carried out as part of a project developed by the Open University's Department of Languages (*Collaborative Writing and Peer Review*) between November 2011 and May 2012. The project was led by the Open University's LORO team and the participants were teachers in the Department of Languages. The teachers who took part in the project were interested in the collaborative production of OERs and in benefiting from each other's expertise and feedback in the field of online and blended language teaching and learning. The authors worked collaboratively in producing a set of online audio-visual materials aimed at helping students of Italian to master the pronunciation of five specific sounds. This process provided an example of how the production and design stage of OERs (which involved goal-setting, planning, researching and designing activities) benefited from openness and sharing. This case study is addressed to members of the online teaching community who are interested in the sharing of resources, practices and intellectual capital as a means to enhance professional development and raise individual tutors' and institutional profiles.

Keywords: peer-reviewing, professional development, online learning and teaching, open access resources, Jing, Italian, collaborative writing, OER, LORO, pronunciation.

1. The Open University in the West Midlands, UK; a.calvi@open.ac.uk

2. The Open University in London, UK; a.motzo@open.ac.uk

3. The Open University in Wales, UK; s.silipo@open.ac.uk

How to cite this chapter: Calvi, A., Motzo, A., & Silipo, S. (2013). Designing OERs to Teach Italian Pronunciation in an Open Educational Environment: A Case Study. In A. Beaven, A. Comas-Quinn, & B. Sawhill (Eds), *Case Studies of Openness in the Language Classroom* (pp. 70-82). © Research-publishing.net.

1. The context

This section describes the institutional context and the specific project within which the authors collaboratively worked to produce a set of Italian language OERs.

1.1. The OU

The OU is a UK-wide Higher Education institution that offers distance tuition to adult (16+) learners. The Department of Languages currently offers language courses in French, German and Spanish (up to degree level) as well as Italian, Chinese, Welsh and English for Academic Purposes. All these modules offer blended tuition, i.e. a mixture of face-to-face group tutorials and online group tutorials (delivered through a synchronous video-conferencing tool). Learners and teachers can also get in contact via online asynchronous tools such as forums, wikis and blogs. Beginners' modules run for 11 months, while modules at other levels run for 8 months. During this time learners submit their assignments electronically via the university's own e-system, and receive electronic feedback from their teachers. Tools used to provide feedback include Audacity and Jing.

1.2. The teachers

Teachers are expected to take active part in the production of materials to be used in the face-to-face and online tutorials. They typically adapt or create online teaching resources (consistent with the programme followed by the course book) to be used on the synchronous video-conferencing tool, and are also encouraged to upload and share their resources on LORO (*Languages Open Resources Online*), an online repository for storing, sharing and accessing language-teaching resources.

1.3. The collaborative writing and peer review project

The main purpose of the project was to give language teachers the opportunity to work collaboratively to produce and share new language-specific OERs, or adapt the existing ones. They were encouraged to exploit a range of synchronous and asynchronous tools (synchronous video-conferencing tool, forum, and emails, Audacity, Jing and Power Point) both for communication purposes and for the creation or re-adaptation of the educational resources. The objective was to share and publish the resources produced by each group by uploading them on an open repository.

Quite early on in the project emphasis was put on the crucial role that peer review has in a collaborative work. Therefore, in the initial phase all project team members worked together in establishing the main rules of working collaboratively in an online environment and produced a 'Netiquette' for peer review.

In a second phase, participants were invited to form different groups and agree on a specific task depending on their common interests and areas of expertise, and on the choice of tool. At this stage, the forum became a lively platform in which useful information, ideas and comments were shared amongst all the participants. Thanks to its openness, participants could interact with members of other groups and ideas emerged easily.

During the production phase, different groups explored different working tools. For effective communication, members preferred emails and regular online conference meetings via synchronous video-conferencing tools (either Elluminate or Skype). The choice of tools used to create or adapt resources depended mainly on the type of resources the group meant to produce.

1.4.   The Italian project

The group consisted of three teachers who had been involved in the delivery of the blended OU Italian Beginners' module L195 'Andante' for five years and Italian Intermediate module L150 'Vivace' for two years.

Each member was able to contribute a variety of relevant skills which she aspired to develop further. Anna Calvi had gathered experience as online language teacher and writer of Italian and EAP materials for online, distance and face-to-face environments. Anna Motzo was an experienced face-to-face and online teacher of Italian who had coached opera singers, and whose areas of interest were pronunciation, production of learning material and e-learning. Sandra Silipo had worked for many years as a teacher of Italian (both face-to-face and online) as well as an author of Italian books, and was particularly interested in improving her online teaching skills and developing resources for the teaching of pronunciation.

2.   Intended outcomes

This section describes the needs of online and distance language learners, the needs of learners of Italian regarding phonology and the specific intended outcomes of the Italian project.

2.1.   The learners' needs

The materials produced by participants to the project were intended to address the specific needs of online and distance learners. Studying a language through a distance course offers learners the advantage of working at their own pace, but challenges are also present. The main challenge that learners face is limited access to face-to-face contact with their teacher and with proficient speakers of the language. This can negatively affect the development of speaking skills and, in particular, pronunciation. There is little time to work on learners' pronunciation during the tutorials, and once the tutorial is over, learners can no longer access a live model. In addition to this, not all learners attend tutorials, which are not compulsory. Particularly affected are learners who have a learning disability and need explicit explanations, a multi-sensory approach and more opportunities for practice.

2.2.   Five challenging Italian sounds

An area which learners of Italian find particularly challenging is the pronunciation of the phonemes [ʎ], [z], [s], [ʃ], and the double consonant /ll/. As can be seen in Table 1, these sounds are difficult to learn either because the sounds do not exist in the English language, or because they exist but are spelt in a different way.

Table 1.   Difficulties faced by English speakers learning to pronounce [ʎ], [z], [s], [ʃ], and the double consonant /ll/

Phonemes	Difficulties
[ʎ] (spelt /gl/)	It does not exist in English (an approximation of it is the phoneme [lj] as in the English word 'million').
[z]	It exists both in Italian and in English, but in English is spelt /z/, while in Italian is spelt /s/.
[s]	It exists in English and is spelt /s/. In Italian spelling /s/ corresponds either to phoneme [z] or phoneme [s] (depending on the position in the word, on the phonemes that precede or follow it and also on regional variations).
[ʃ]	It exists in English but has a different spelling from the Italian (English /sh/, Italian /sci/, /sce/).
The double consonant sound /ll/	It does not exist in English

2.3.   Intended outcomes of the Italian project

The goal was to produce resources which would help learners of Italian to improve their pronunciation of individual phonemes. The aim was therefore to design materials that would:

- help learners to recognize and pronounce the phonemes [ʎ], [z], [s], [ʃ], and the double consonant /ll/;

- provide them with easily accessible explanations and opportunities for practice.

Another goal was to develop professionally and improve support techniques. It was therefore hoped that as a result of the project the authors would be better able to:

- prepare learners for oral assignments;

- provide effective feedback on assignments;

- produce multimodal materials involving the use of sound and visuals (images and text);

- use Jing in combination with PowerPoint;

- work collaboratively with colleagues.

Overall, the authors felt that the project would help them become more autonomous not only in their effort to develop professionally but also in their ability to produce materials that suit their teaching styles and learners' needs.

Finally, the authors also wanted their project to have a wider impact, so they planned to produce resources that could:

- contribute to the delivery of the Italian beginners and intermediate modules;

- constitute an example of good practice and attract useful feedback;

- be made available to our OU colleagues and the wider teaching community.

3.   Nuts and bolts

The authors started by discussing which tools would best help them to meet their goals. They agreed that the best way to produce multimodal materials incorporating sound and visuals would be to create a PowerPoint presentation and incorporate it in Jing before uploading it on LORO.

PowerPoint is a versatile tool normally used in both face-to-face and online tutorials. PP presentations can be easily uploaded on Elluminate and can also be easily shared with learners if they want to go over the language they have practised during a tutorial.

Jing is a screencasting computer program launched in 2007 by the TechSmith Corporation. The software takes a picture or video (image and sound) of the user's computer screen and uploads it to the Web. When the pictures or videos are uploaded to the web, Jing automatically creates a URL that can be shared with others. There are several reasons why Jing fitted in with the authors' objectives: it has a simple format, is user-friendly and is compatible with both Macintosh and Microsoft Windows. Users must sign up for an account before using the software, but registration is free, and there is no need to register and/or download the software in order to access the URL. All that learners need to do in order to access a recording is click on a link to open a web page. Jing recordings can be uploaded and shared on LORO, can be shared via their web link, and can be opened on Elluminate.

4.　　In practice:
　　Three Italian tongue twisters

After agreeing which tools would be used, the project group members had to choose the content of the recordings: a short text (Jing recordings cannot be more than 5 minutes long) which could be used as a basis for pronunciation practice.

Tongue twisters were used for three reasons. First of all, in Italy tongue twisters are commonly used in primary schools to teach children specific spellings and the related sounds, and to help them to develop fluency. Tongue twisters also stimulate repetition which in turn helps learners to acquire confidence and develop fluency. Finally, tongue twisters are motivating as they bring an element of fun to the learning process, as well as an insight into Italian culture.

Three relevant tongue twisters were selected and each author created a PowerPoint presentation focussing on one of them. The presentation was then recorded on Jing, and the URLs of the material produced were posted on the project forum. This allowed the authors to edit their work thanks to valuable feedback and comments from their colleagues. Finally, the resources were uploaded on LORO so that they could be accessed by colleagues.

The three presentations (La pronuncia della lettera 's'; Double consonants in Italian: a tongue-twister; Pronouncing the Italian sound 'gl') are similarly structured, in order to provide consistency, but not identical, because they allow for variation depending on the sounds presented.

The first slide (or set of slides) provides a visual representation of how to move the mouth in order to produce the selected sound. A voice-over explains how to produce the selected sounds (see Figure 1).

Figure 1.   How to articulate the sound

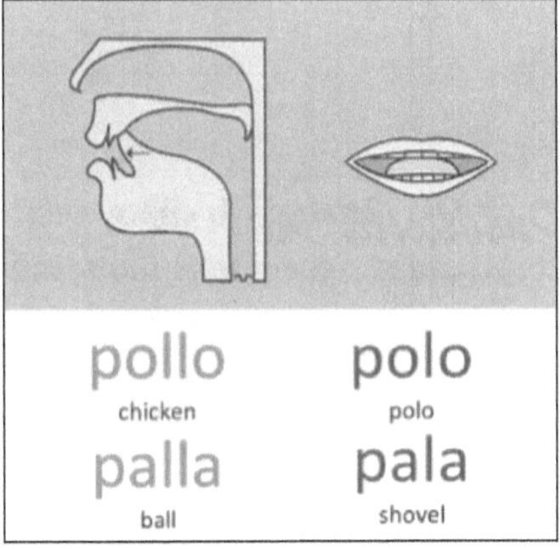

The second slide (or set of slides) provides words from the tongue twisters which contain the different selected sounds. A voice-over reads the words (see Figure 2).

Figure 2.   Examples from the tongue twister

If necessary, the different sounds presented are compared in a new slide with both a visual and an auditory stimulus (see Figure 3).

Figure 3.   Comparison of sounds

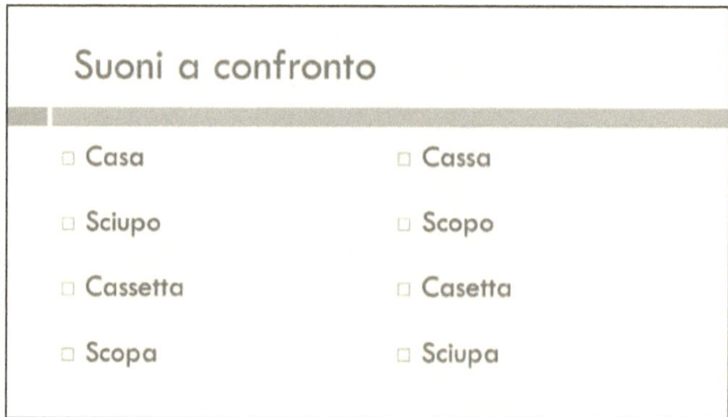

The whole tongue twister is introduced line by line, together with a visual aid (either drawing or picture) which illustrates and encapsulates the tongue twister through an image (see Figure 4).

Figure 4.   The tongue twister

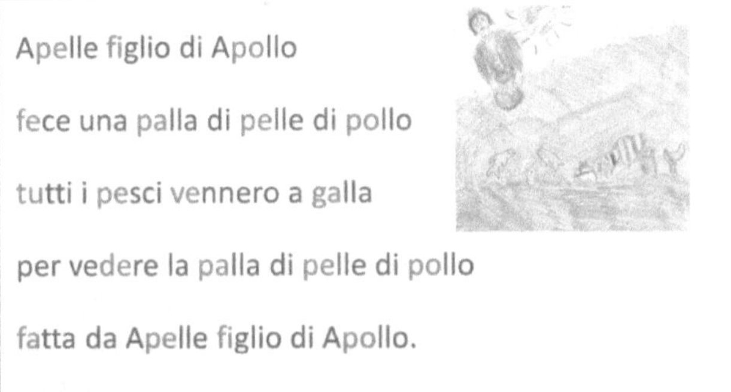

The final slide provides the translation in English (see Figure 5).

Figure 5.   Translation of the tongue twister

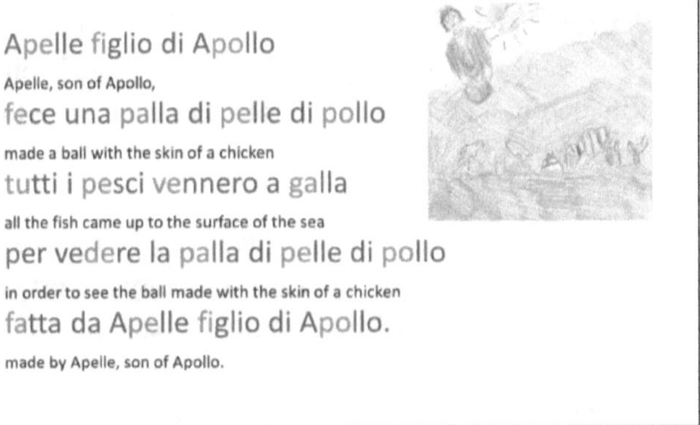

Two members of the group used the resources in their tutorials. In one case the teacher presented them in a face-to-face tutorial (using PowerPoint) and then sent the URL of the Jing videos to the learners so that they could practise again on their own. In the other case, the activity was carried out online by uploading the Jing video on Elluminate. The learners were then encouraged to save it for practice and to record their voice using Audacity or another audio recording facility.

5.   Conclusion

This collaborative experience can be evaluated in terms of the resources created, the process adopted and the professional skills and understandings gained by its participants.

5.1.   The resources

The resources produced constitute a good example of OERs. From a pedagogical point of view, they have a clear objective and this is relevant to teachers teaching an Italian course to English speakers as they focus on difficulties that English speakers generally face.

They are free and easily accessible through the LORO repository and re-usable by other teachers within and outside the university. Teachers can also choose to use them as templates when they design their own presentations and draw inspiration from them to develop similar resources to support learners of other languages. Although resources uploaded on LORO are not formally evaluated by module teams, users are encouraged to post their comments on them.

The resources were created under the Creative Commons Attribution Only Licence principle which means users are free to modify the original material, provided that the creator is acknowledged, and they can be modified because other users can access the PowerPoint presentation and use it as a template to create their own resource. In addition, other users can vary the way in which the resources are exploited to promote learning. For instance, both the PowerPoint slides and Jing videos can be made available to learners through a range of online environments and applications such as websites, online classrooms, tutor group forums, e-mails and e-feedback as well as face-to-face lessons.

Finally, the materials are also interactive in that the learner is encouraged to repeat after the teacher and, as they follow a multi-modal approach, they are likely to appeal to many learners and more effectively support language learning.

5.2.   The collaborative process

In terms of the collaborative process, the experience has been successful. The authors have relied on peer review as a quality assurance tool and have been able to fully exploit their different competences and therefore have complemented each other in every stage of the process. Competences included the ability to teach pronunciation and use Jing as well as the ability to create resources, or to find and adapt openly licensed resources such as resource books, drawings and pictures.

The process was successful as participants were willing to join and to participate in an open and fruitful dialogue: each member contributed by providing ideas, support and mutual encouragement. The participants soon understood that, as individuals, they did not need a comprehensive ability to carry out all tasks since, as members of the group, they were able to motivate and complement each other and also give each other feedback. While this meant being open to criticism and willingness to negotiate, the final product was definitely superior to what they could have done on their own.

Working together has also highlighted how a single template can be successfully customised by the different teachers depending on their teaching styles, considerations of the learners' needs and the choice of pedagogical content. For example, teachers can use the template to focus mainly on the way in which a sound is made or spend more time helping learners to practise its use. Others may prefer a more balanced approach, involving explanations and practice.

5.3.   Professional development

The project has allowed the authors to develop their ability to use technology for educational purposes. Adapting, designing and creating OERs requires a certain degree of familiarity with IT tools and a willingness to experiment with them. Although PowerPoint is a well-known piece of software, and Jing is user-friendly and mostly self-explanatory, it has taken some time, careful planning and several attempts to combine the two successfully.

The authors identified differences between methodologies used in different environments. When teaching pronunciation in a face-to-face situation, teachers rely heavily on visual clues (learners imitate the way teachers move their lips and mouth), and explanations can be tailored to learners' needs. When teaching pronunciation to distance learners through the means of online tools, explanations have to be concise and precise, in order to compensate the lack of visual clues.

Finally the project helped the authors to further extend their roles. Producing OERs with a peer group meant changing the way the authors saw themselves as teachers and gave them the opportunity to develop skills that are not traditionally associated with their role.

Useful links

Audacity software for recording and editing sounds: http://audacity.sourceforge.net/
LORO repository: http://loro.open.ac.uk
JING screen capture tool: http://www.techsmith.com/jing.html
La pronuncia della lettera 's': http://loro.open.ac.uk/2934/
Double consonants in Italian: a tongue-twister: http://loro.open.ac.uk/2859/
Pronouncing the Italian sound 'gl': http://loro.open.ac.uk/3502/

Section 3.

Sharing Practice

FAVORing the Part-time Language Teacher: The Experience and Impact of Sharing Open Educational Resources through a Community-based Repository

Julie Watson[1]

Abstract

The resourcefulness of part-time language teachers is often overlooked, despite the large numbers of such staff teaching in language departments across higher education. Part-time teachers typically juggle life work commitments and experience far fewer opportunities for professional development than their full-time colleagues. They frequently work in relative isolation, yet carry out their teaching duties enthusiastically and conscientiously, striving to provide as rich a learning experience as possible for their students, often spending a considerable amount of time in lesson and resource preparation. The aim of the JISC-funded FAVOR (Find a Voice through Open Resources) Project was to bring more part-time teachers into the open content movement, drawing on their wealth of resourcefulness and offering them something back for all their, often unrecognised, hard work. This case study will describe one participating institution's experience on the FAVOR Project, including an initial investigation into its impact on the post-project practices of part-time teachers. It will draw on a range of qualitative data gathered from individual and group meetings, teacher interviews, and reflective notes made by the institutional coordinator to present a picture of the experience from the part-time teachers' perspective.

Keywords: part-time teachers, OER learning design, adapting for sharing, LOC authoring tool, continuing teacher practice.

1. Principal Teaching Fellow in eLearning, Modern Languages, University of Southampton, UK; J.Watson@soton.ac.uk

How to cite this chapter: Watson, J. (2013). FAVORing the Part-time Language Teacher: The Experience and Impact of Sharing Open Educational Resources through a Community-based Repository. In A. Beaven, A. Comas-Quinn, & B. Sawhill (Eds), *Case Studies of Openness in the Language Classroom* (pp. 85-95). © Research-publishing.net.

1. Context: Background to the FAVOR project

The FAVOR Project (Find a Voice through Open Resources) was an OER (Open Educational Resource) initiative led by the Languages, Linguistics and Area Studies (LLAS) Centre at the University of Southampton and funded through JISC (Joint Information Systems Committee). Its primary aim was to engage part-time teachers of mainstream and lesser-taught languages in higher education and draw on their resourcefulness and experience to both generate and exploit Open Content (OC) for teaching and learning. Additionally, the project aimed to highlight the often unrecognised and undervalued resource that part-time teachers represent within our institutions. Nearly 30 part-time language teachers were coordinated from five UK Higher Education Institutions (Aston University; Newcastle University; School of Oriental and African Studies; University College London – School of Slavonic and East European studies; and the University of Southampton – Modern Languages) and by the end of the project, over 300 existing and created language teaching resources in 17 languages, produced in a range of digital media, had been shared through LanguageBox, an open content repository for language teachers and learners.

At the University of Southampton, five part-time teachers of four mainstream languages (French, German, Italian and ESL/EAP) were recruited and coordinated by the author. The teachers were involved in teaching language levels from beginner through to advanced, which included students on full-time accredited language modules run during the daytime and part-time evening language classes offered through the university's Lifelong Learning programme. The nature of their teaching ranged widely from language conversation classes to intensive EAP summer courses in all language skill areas (reading, writing, listening and speaking).

In the first phase of the project the part-time teachers drew on their existing banks of self-created language learning content for sharing as OER. In the second phase, the teachers designed and created new resources for use with their own classes, learning to use the LOC (Learning Object Creator) authoring tool.

This case study focuses on the particular experiences of the Southampton group of part-time teachers in the project, and their perceptions three months after the project end. It offers a view, mediated by the coordinator (the author), which draws on her reflective notes and qualitative data gathered from individual and group meetings with the teachers. It also summarises some of the findings from data gathered during semi-structured interviews with the teachers after the conclusion of the project. These interviews particularly sought to determine how teachers' participation in the project might have impacted on their practice in the longer term.

2.   Intended outcomes: Drawing in and drawing out the part-time teacher

There were several intended outcomes of the FAVOR Project.

By specifically engaging with part-time teachers, the project sought to draw in and recognise the value of these teachers in the context of the OC movement as well as realise some of the advantages of open practice among the group members. Such teachers often find themselves on the periphery of academic departments and separated both from each other as well as from colleagues in the mainstream teaching community. This situation arises for a variety of reasons, but, as one participant noted:

> *"Part-time language tutors do not spend lots of time in the university; for some, the only time (they spend) there is for teaching – some tutors do not even have a desk and a computer."*

Working in relative isolation, these teachers have little opportunity for professional development even informally through exchange of ideas, mutual support and colleague interaction. Any innovative ideas or lessons that they may produce are noticed only by their students and their reward for these lies simply in the satisfaction of a lesson that was well received and achieved its teaching objectives.

Teachers volunteered to participate and so were self-selected for the project. However, despite the intended outcome, several admitted to some initial scepticism about what they would be able to gain from involvement in the project or, at least, put into practice in the longer term:

> *"Before the project, I had nothing to do with e-learning and I had quite a few prejudices concerning e-learning. I always thought of it as red eyes and repetitive exercises... the system crashing down on me while I was trying to do it in class. That (apprehension) has all gone completely!"*

In other circumstances, with their often busy agendas, juggling other commitments (e.g. young children; doctoral studies) and general lack of visibility even when on campus, this group of teachers are normally among the last to be reached in terms of new ideas or practices, especially if these might add to their workloads. Through involvement with FAVOR, these part-time teachers might become relatively 'early adopters' in the OC movement whereas without the project they might be difficult to reach.

The creation of a self-supporting community was also a hoped for outcome of the project, enabling teachers such as these to make and maintain contact with each other and develop a portfolio of OER together – learning from each other at the same time as developing confidence and awareness of what they could offer (and receive) through engagement in open practice.

3.   Nuts and bolts: Tools, training and support

At the outset, the teachers created accounts in LanguageBox, the public repository used for storing and sharing the OER, and a personal profile page, which enabled them to establish their professional credentials and interests within the LanguageBox user community. They were supported through this process by the coordinator, an experienced LanguageBox user. For most, this action represented their first step in developing a professional presence online. By publishing some of their teaching and learning material as open content, these teachers could also 'find a voice' (*"It's going out into the public with my name on it"*) and begin to build their own professional profiles, both through the online presence they created in LanguageBox (and in some cases through subsequent conference and workshop participation).

The teachers were then guided through identifying existing self-created language learning content to share as OER. They received technical training in adapting, if required, and uploading these resources to LanguageBox and adding the necessary metadata, including the use of a 'FAVOR' and 'UKOER' tag for all project outputs, to enhance the 'discoverability' of their resources by others. Interestingly, some of the teachers even began to experiment with new tools to extend the range of media for these OER:

> *"For example, the PowerPoint – I never used them before. I now have an idea how to do it. I'm using some more now for grammar – new ones that I made. It's opened a new path for me."*

In the second phase, the teachers received training as a group in the use of the online LOC authoring tool to enable them to create OER from scratch. The LOC tool, designed and built through a collaborative endeavour at the University of Southampton, is being successfully used, particularly by language teachers, all over the UK and is a teacher-friendly authoring tool, with an explicit learning design for creating online resources in the form of interactive learning objects. It also comprises a pedagogic planning template, which supports teachers through the transition from designing learning activities for the face-to-face class to designing them for online use. This feature proved to be a particular attraction for the teachers (see Section 3). The coordinator provided regular feedback on teachers' draft plans for their 'Learning Objects', which enabled them to consolidate their LOC training and make progress with planning and creating new resources. She also trained teachers in uploading LOC tool outputs to LanguageBox.

Besides the sharing and creation of language-focused OER in a range of digital media, the project fostered a language teacher community of practice through *the process* of sharing and creating teaching resources, with LanguageBox acting as the focal share-point. This was evidenced when online groups began to spring up, creating networks of part-time teachers of the same language, at the same institution, or with a shared thematic or cultural interest (see Section 4).

4.   In practice: Learning with each other and from each other

During the first phase of the project, in the course of initial group discussions about how and what to select to share from their existing banks of resources, teachers had decided that they wanted to adapt their OER in ways to make them more flexible for new users (e.g. by adding transcripts; tasks; suggestions for users). This was not a requirement; however, teachers modified many of their resources as they saw necessary, feeling the need to *"...think carefully whether it needs to be improved"* or made more suitable for reuse as OC. Only once these modifications had been made, were the resources felt to be ready for uploading to LanguageBox.

A University of Southampton FAVOR group was established within LanguageBox, allowing all of the teachers' uploads to be showcased in one place. Groups of teachers representing other universities in the project created similar groups. In addition to this, language- and topic-specific sub-groups also began to spring up (e.g. the Condividiamo (Italian) group; the Horn of Africa Project group; the Swahili Interest group) (see Figure 1). These 'resource aggregating' actions helped all teacher participants in the project, locally or nationally dispersed, to track and view recent project uploads and colleague activity through the shared focal point of LanguageBox, thus fostering the development of the wider FAVOR community.

For many participants, this phase had also represented an opportunity to develop greater technological awareness and enhance their technical skill base, through introduction to the concept of OER and shared repositories, and also by learning to repurpose their existing teaching content in a wider range of formats (see Figure 2).

Figure 1.   Three of the topic-specific groups in LanguageBox
that grew out of the FAVOR project

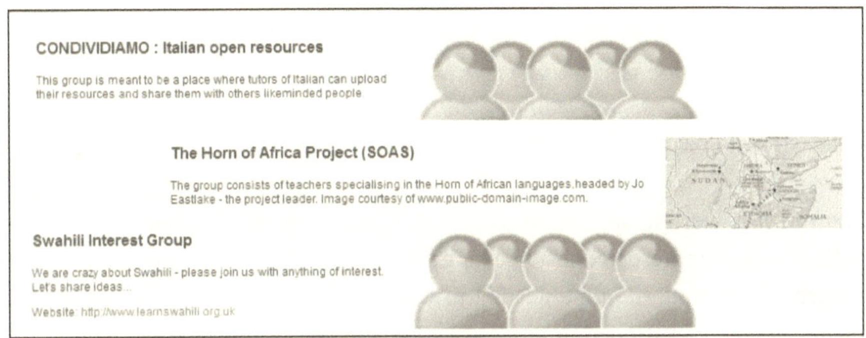

Figure 2.   A participant's repurposed resource as a PowerPoint presentation
for teaching basic description in French

In the next phase, the teachers had received training in the use of the LOC
authoring tool for creating new online teaching and learning resources. Post-
project interviews with the part-time teachers highlighted exactly how useful

the tool's embedded pedagogic support, especially the planning sheet, had been at this stage:

> *"What really helped is the [LOC planning] template..., [which] really impacted on the way I approach lessons. I'm not a language teacher by training; my degree is in translation, then Applied Linguistics. I had a lot of teaching experience but zero pedagogical training."*

Learning to design and build online language learning resources with an authoring tool represented a step change for the teachers, as well as a challenge in terms of finding the time needed to commit to this phase. Nevertheless, all persevered and succeeded in producing thoughtfully-designed and activity-rich learning objects in their respective language teaching fields. The extent to which they had learned from each other as a community was also particularly noted by participants in the post-project interviews:

> *"I've looked at someone else's approach to teaching and then created my own resource from it."*

> *"X had this idea how to deal with a text. It struck me as a really good idea. I'm thinking about it – is there a way to adapt it?"*

> *"It's helped improve the quality of the resources I use... given me an opportunity to think about how I use resources and how others use resources."*

In practice, the use of LanguageBox as a focal point for the project allowed part-time teachers to share not only their OER but also their ideas.

5.   Conclusion

5.1.   Preliminary evaluation

Besides the community-derived benefits, two major gains from the project were felt to be the teachers' engagement with new technological tools for delivering online language learning content (from simple PowerPoint to more complex Learning Object outputs), and the pedagogical gain from revisiting learning design through the LOC planning template and reflection about the reuse of the pedagogic approaches underpinning others' resources.

On one level, sharing teaching resources as OC only has meaning if others choose to reuse or repurpose them. This ultimate goal may not occur within the time confines of a project. However, as found in other OER initiatives, the benefits, and specifically, our understanding of the concepts of reuse and repurposing, do not have to be understood solely in terms of the actual online resources (e.g. Beaven, 2013).

The three-month post-project interviews shed some important insights into the question of resource reuse and repurposing. Three of the five teachers acknowledged having reused their own resources, while the other two reused those of others. Unsuitability of some of their created OER for the levels of the classes currently being taught was noted, and no repurposing had occurred due to lack of time at the start of the academic year. However, all participants mentioned the fact that they had 'reused' or adapted ideas or approaches that they had found underpinning the resources of others. Some also mentioned abstracting pedagogic principles and practices embedded in the LOC planning template:

> *"I have recycled ideas and targeted them towards my own students – no group is alike; I always find I need to retarget... I look for ideas more than for the actual resources."*

> *"What I reused is this format because I really like that very much... I started being very aware of structure – at the beginning I had material sitting at home so I would just restructure it using the template, but then later I would go online looking for ideas... I take ideas from bits and pieces that are relevant to mine but change them."*

This teacher went on to explain how she repurposed the teaching approach used in another teacher's German language picture story about the process of producing Christmas baubles, which required students to interpret and retell to each other in stages. She repurposed and extended the idea in the form of a German advent calendar requiring students to create a story around the pictures revealed each day. As she said, *"the original gave me the idea"*.

The participants all cited their exposure to the design patterns implicit in the ideas of others as a particularly useful way in which the project had supported their teacher development. Pedagogic benefit was also noted to have impacted on classroom practice (i.e. reapplying LOC learning design principles when lesson planning).

5.2.   Concluding remarks

Time will tell how far the teaching resources shared and created during FAVOR will be reused and repurposed by others; nevertheless, it was clearly stated to be the intention of the teachers themselves to do this when the right class arose and time permitted. The teachers' increased confidence in their own professionalism and development of a positive attitude towards sharing and benefiting from OC were highlighted.

Teacher gain in terms of increased sensitisation to the 'idea template' or 'learning design' inherent in their own OER and those of other people may ultimately be the most important outcome of this project. In this regard, FAVOR outcomes are in line with those of other OER initiatives (e.g. Borthwick, 2013; McGill, Beetham, Falconer, & Littlejohn, 2010), proving that what we are discovering, as we move into the world of OC and practice, turns out to be a much richer experience than what we originally expected.

Acknowledgement. I would like to thank Bianca, Denise, Katy, Livia and Lucie, the part-time tutors at University of Southampton, for all their work in the FAVOR Project and for giving me permission to quote them.

Useful links

FAVOR Project: https://www.llas.ac.uk//sites/default/files/nodes/6505/FAVOR-Final-report.pdf

LLAS: https://www.llas.ac.uk

JISC: http://www.jisc.ac.uk/

LanguageBox: http://languagebox.ac.uk/

LOC: http://loc.llas.ac.uk/

Condividiamo group: http://languagebox.ac.uk/group/26

Horn of Africa Project group: http://languagebox.ac.uk/group/17

Swahili Interest group: http://languagebox.ac.uk/group/20

References

Beaven, T. (2013). Use and Reuse of OER: professional conversations with language teachers. *Journal of e-Learning and Knowledge Society, 9*(1) 59-71. Retrieved from http://www.jelks.org/ojs/index.php/Je-LKS_EN/article/view/802

Borthwick, K. (2013). *The FAVOR Project Final Report*. Retrieved from http://www.llas.ac.uk/sites/default/files/nodes/6505/FAVOR-Final-report.pdf

McGill, L., Beetham, H., Falconer, I., & Littlejohn, A. (2010). *JISC/HE Academy OER Programme: Pilot Phase Synthesis and Evaluation Report*. Retrieved from https://oersynth.pbworks.com/w/page/29688444/Pilot%20Phase%20Synthesis%20and%20Evaluation%20Report

8 The Community Café: Open Practice with Community-based Language Teachers

Kate Borthwick[1] and Alison Dickens[2]

Abstract

This case study describes the work of the Community Café project, which ran from 2010-2011. The project's aim was to foster a community of open practice amongst community-based language teachers by encouraging them to create and publish open educational resources related to their teaching, on an open community repository. The project aimed to address the scarcity of up-to-date, online resources for community languages; the lack of training for Community-based teachers in ICT or innovative pedagogy, and the isolated nature of working in informal, community-based settings. This study considers and outlines the practical steps which were taken to set up the project and engage the community group, who were new to open educational resources and open practice. It describes the mix of informal meetings and formal teacher training employed by the project, and also the issues that need to be considered when reaching out to an ethnically diverse community group. It also gives practical examples of how teachers engaged with project tasks and open educational practice. It concludes that open working has the potential to have a significant impact on the professional lives of community-based language teachers, but that such teachers need time to absorb and embed new knowledge effectively.

Keywords: open educational resources, community languages, professional development, open educational practice, repositories, teaching.

1. Centre for Languages, Linguistics and Area Studies, University of Southampton, UK; K.Borthwick@soton.ac.uk

2. Centre for Languages, Linguistics and Area Studies, University of Southampton, UK; A.M.Dickens@soton.ac.uk

How to cite this chapter: Borthwick, K., & Dickens, A. (2013). The Community Café: Open Practice with Community-based Language Teachers. In A. Beaven, A. Comas-Quinn, & B. Sawhill (Eds), *Case Studies of Openness in the Language Classroom* (pp. 96-109). © Research-publishing.net.

1.   Context

This case study describes the work of the UK JISC-funded Community Café project, which ran from 2010-2011 (JISC is the Joint Information Systems Committee, a charity which supports technology in education). This project was a collaboration between the University of Southampton, Southampton City Council, and Manchester Metropolitan University, and its aim was to foster a community of open practice amongst community-based language teachers by encouraging them to create and publish open educational resources related to their teaching, on an open community repository.

Community languages are "…languages spoken by members of minority groups or communities within a majority language context" (CILT, The National Centre for Languages). Such languages are often taught 'out-of-hours': in evenings and at weekends in supplementary schools. The teachers of these languages are frequently volunteers and either receive no remuneration or are paid a low hourly rate by local government authorities. They often have no formal teacher training but are native speakers of the languages they teach, and are motivated by enthusiasm, a love of their language and culture, and a desire for the young people in their community to maintain language skills.

Most teach in addition to maintaining full-time jobs or family commitments, and have limited access to on-going training or resources, and limited time for preparation. Yet they face challenging teaching environments, typically having to deal with diverse class sizes, as well as diverse age ranges and abilities frequently within a single class. There is often a lack of appropriate resources for the language that they teach and so most teachers are reliant on creating their own materials.

In the Southampton area, a wide range of community languages are spoken, including Polish, Bengali, Afghan Farsi, Italian and Chinese. Many of these languages are taught to GCSE and A level (UK public examinations taken at the age of 16 and 18 respectively) and pupils range from small children to adult learners. Community-based language teaching within Southampton is coordinated by the City Council, who apportions a small amount of funding towards maintaining a network of community-based language teachers. This funding does not include training or resource development.

The Centre for Languages, Linguistics and Area Studies (LLAS), based at the University of Southampton, have been working with language teachers in higher education to explore the benefits and challenges of OEP for several years, and LLAS maintains an open community repository called LanguageBox. The authors identified OEP and publication of OERs as having potential as low-cost, self-sustaining initiatives which could improve the professional lives of community-based language teachers and address many of the challenging issues which they face. Community-based language teachers often do not have access to the tools, knowledge and experience available in mainstream sectors of education. The Community Café project would seek to bridge this gap.

2.   Intended outcomes

The project initially set out to collect and co-create a suite of digital resources for community language teaching and learning and to publish them as open content on a community website. This would increase the pool of suitable, up-to-date, digital content available to teachers and learners. However, we had other key aims:

- to build a self-managed community-based group (online and offline) to support people engaged in teaching and learning the range of community languages available locally in Southampton;

- to improve the pedagogy of existing materials and methods through peer review and discussion, and encourage general reflective practice;

- to provide bespoke training in using, creating, publishing and sharing digital content;

- to contribute to the enhancement of the profile and provision of community language learning through adding resources to an online repository hosting a wide range of language resources used in all UK education sectors;

- to open up connections and strengthen existing relationships between academic departments and the local community (both in Southampton and in other geographical locations taking part in the project).

Our intention was to use the publication of open educational resources to offer professional development opportunities to community-based teachers and to encourage enhanced practice through sharing work within a community of peers. The ethos of open working and the 'OER movement' is one of collegiality and sharing across traditional boundaries and we felt that this was highly relevant to teachers working in isolation, outside of mainstream educational settings. It is satisfying and rewarding to share ideas with and learn from colleagues; however, community languages teachers rarely have the opportunity to meet each other. An online community enables networking and sharing to happen within a professional space that is flexible and accommodating and can be accessed at any time and from any location.

The authors used the LLAS community repository, the LanguageBox, as the online space for sharing resources. This site has a social networking aspect and allows for the creation of personal profiles, the addition of comments to resources, emails to resource-creators via the system, and is appealing and easy to use. It already hosts a wide range of resources contributed by teachers from all sectors of education in a range of languages, and could therefore offer our community language teacher group a voice within a wider community of practice, and exposure to different types of resources and ideas.

In this way, the project intended to bring the knowledge, experience, tools and equipment available in the HE sector to assist community-based teachers in improving their practice. Offline (face-to-face) training in the use of technology for teaching and in creating OERs would be essential in order for our teachers to access this knowledge and experience, and the contacts and organisational networks of Southampton City Council would also be essential in attracting teachers to the project and maintaining communications with them.

3.   Nuts and bolts

3.1.   Communications

The project team was fortunate in being able to use the existing Community Languages support network, coordinated by Southampton City Council, to introduce and recruit teachers to the project. The council officer who ran the network was personally acquainted with all of the teachers, and used every means available to make contact with them (e.g. email, fax, telephone, letter). This range of communication methods was essential as it could accommodate different levels of English language knowledge, and different preferences for communication with the outside world. The use of an existing contact and network was crucial in recruiting and then supporting teachers throughout the project.

3.2.   Informal, 'café' meetings

The project proceeded with a mixture of informal, café-style meetings and more formal training sessions. The idea behind the Café meetings was that they would provide a forum for 'offline' discussion and would complement the workshops offering training in the use of technology for teaching and sharing. The Café sessions were intentionally informal and user-centred in nature, to enable participants to feel comfortable, to encourage conversations across language groupings, to build confidence in creating digital resources and in using English to describe teaching methods and resources, and to overcome any reticence in sharing ideas/practices. Meetings always featured lots of tea/coffee drinking and cake consumption (carrot cake being a particular favourite).

Café sessions were held at a local school in Southampton, which is the usual venue for meetings of the Community Languages Network. Meetings were necessarily held 'out-of-hours' because this is the only time that the teachers were available. Our initial intention was to use a more laid-back local, a public venue such as a café or a library, but participants were clear in their preference for a familiar location.

The first session was designed with the idea of getting teachers to join the project, but also to encourage them to have input into the shape of future meetings. The project team were keen that participants should feel a sense of ownership in the project, and that activities should be directly relevant and responsive to their needs as teachers. We felt that this would increase the likelihood for success, as well as increasing the chances of future sustainability for teacher engagement with open practice and OERs. Subsequent meetings were held every month, on a Tuesday evening.

The structure of each café session was flexible but usually revolved around discussion and practice sharing. Meetings were led by members of the project team, who would typically introduce a theme (e.g. 'using interactive materials in teaching') and encourage participants to mix with new acquaintances cross-language groupings. The themes covered in cafe meetings were chosen to complement the training workshops and to prepare participants for the practical sessions. This ensured that pedagogical ideas, language issues, and concepts around open working could be worked through in advance, enabling trainers to focus on practical issues during workshops.

3.3.   Training sessions

Six evening workshops in the use of technology in language teaching ran during the course of the project. They were held at the University of Southampton and were facilitated either by members of LLAS or by commissioned trainers. Topics were negotiated with tutors at the outset of the project and were on these areas: using and sharing material on the LanguageBox, creating podcasts, using *Powerpoint* for language teaching, creating online activities using *Hot Potatoes* – part 1, creating online activities using *Hot Potatoes* – part 2, and tips for teaching diverse groups. There were also several unstructured sessions during which participants worked on material of their choice. The workshops were practical and offered participants hands-on experience with tools and software.

4. In practice

Workshop sessions were structured around an achievable task so that each participant was able to complete a digital item by the end of the workshop. The reasoning behind this design was that it was intended to encourage a sense of achievement and empowerment in the group. Workshop tasks were kept consciously simple in order to accommodate all levels of IT-literacy or English language issues. However, tasks were flexible enough to allow for adaptation and extension by those who felt more confident in their resource-creation.

The following examples illustrate how two Community Café themes worked in practice.

4.1. Podcasting/creating audio recordings for teaching

The café session preceding the practical workshop prepared the participants to create their own online audio recordings to use in class. The session encouraged discussion around why creating audio recordings could be useful; how audio material can be presented, and some basic principles related to creating audio recordings. It concluded with participants creating a plan and script for a short audio recording. Figure 1, Figure 2 and Figure 3 below show an extract from the facilitator's notes and the plans made by a teacher of Punjabi for an audio recording on the topic of 'summer'.

During the practical workshop which followed this café session, participants learned how to use the free audio recording software, *Audacity*, and then went on to create their own recordings. Figure 4 shows the final online open recording on the topic of 'summer', in Punjabi. This file on the LanguageBox includes the plans illustrated above.

Figure 1.   An extract from the Facilitator's notes for the café session on podcasting http://languagebox.ac.uk/1854/

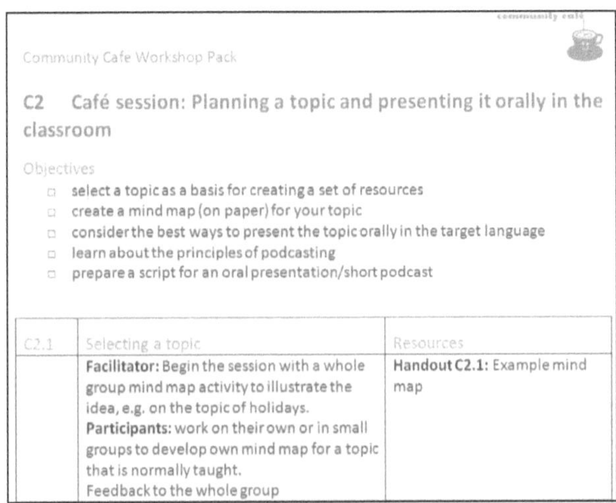

Community Cafe Workshop Pack

C2   Café session: Planning a topic and presenting it orally in the classroom

Objectives

- select a topic as a basis for creating a set of resources
- create a mind map (on paper) for your topic
- consider the best ways to present the topic orally in the target language
- learn about the principles of podcasting
- prepare a script for an oral presentation/short podcast

C2.1	Selecting a topic	Resources
	Facilitator: Begin the session with a whole group mind map activity to illustrate the idea, e.g. on the topic of holidays. **Participants:** work on their own or in small groups to develop own mind map for a topic that is normally taught. Feedback to the whole group	Handout C2.1: Example mind map

Figure 2.   The script for the audio recording in Punjabi, on the topic of 'summer' http://languagebox.ac.uk/1779/

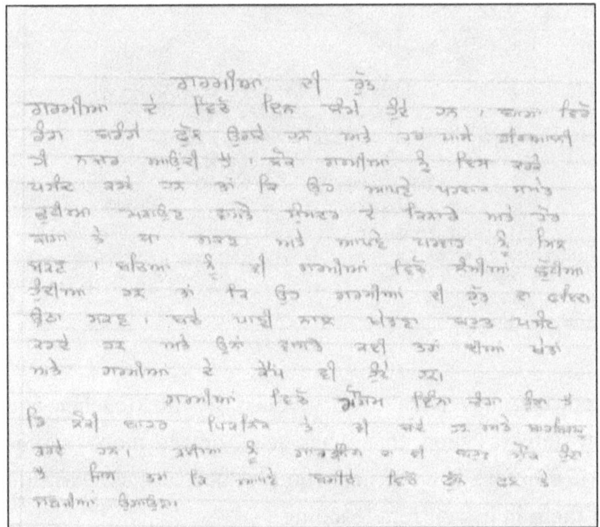

Figure 3.   A plan for a recording on the topic of 'summer',
in Punjabi http://languagebox.ac.uk/1779/

Community Café: Creating a podcast

Name:	
Language(s) taught:	Punjabi
Age(s) of learners:	10 -15

Level(s) of learners:	Beginners	Intermediate	Advanced	Mixed ability
		X		

Idea for podcast(s):	Summer
What do you need to create your podcast? (just you? Music? Other people? Sounds?)	

Language skill that the podcast supports:	Reading	Writing	Speaking	Listening	Grammar	Vocabulary
			X	X	X	X

Keywords:	
Script for your podcast (continue on other side):	Translation: Summer has long sunny days. Summer is colourful as there are many different colours of flowers and green all around. People like summer because they can go on family trips to the beach and other places to visit like the countryside. They also like to visit their families. Children have long summer holidays so they can enjoy the hot weather. They love playing with water guns and having water fights. There are lots of activities for children during their summer holidays. Children enjoy going to funfairs and camping. People have lots of barbecues and picnics because the weather is so nice. Some people like gardening and growing flowers, fruit and vegetables. You can hear birds singing early in the morning. Summer is an enjoyable season for everyone.

The final recording has been used in class by the teacher concerned, and LanguageBox statistics show that it has been viewed more than 350 times and downloaded 178 times. The teacher who produced it has learnt new skills and makes use of them in her current teaching.

Figure 4.   An audio recording on the topic of 'summer',
in Punjabi, with accompanying files
http://languagebox.ac.uk/1779/

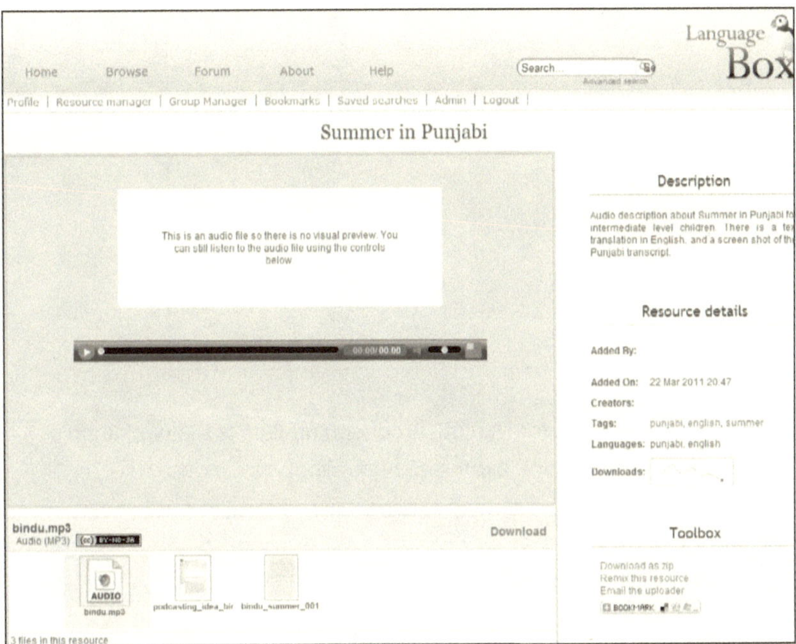

4.2.   Creating an online quiz/game

The café session related to the creation of quizzes and games for language teaching involved discussion and consideration of how teachers use games and why they can be useful. The session concluded with the planning and preparation of a quiz which could then be put into free *Hot Potatoes* software to make an interactive online exercise. During the workshop, participants learnt how to use the free software *Hot Potatoes*, including how to change colours and insert images. Figure 5 and Figure 6 show an extract from the planning sheet which participants' used and one of the quizzes produced during the workshop.

Figure 5. Planning sheet for creating an online quiz http://languagebox.ac.uk/1858/

Community Café Workshop Pack

Handout C4.4

Quiz Planning Sheet

Topic:				
Title:				
Question 1:				
Answer choices:	a)	b)	c)	d)
Image (note link)				
Feedback:	Correct Answer		Incorrect Answers	
Question 2:				
Answer choices:	a)	b)	c)	d)
Image (note link)				

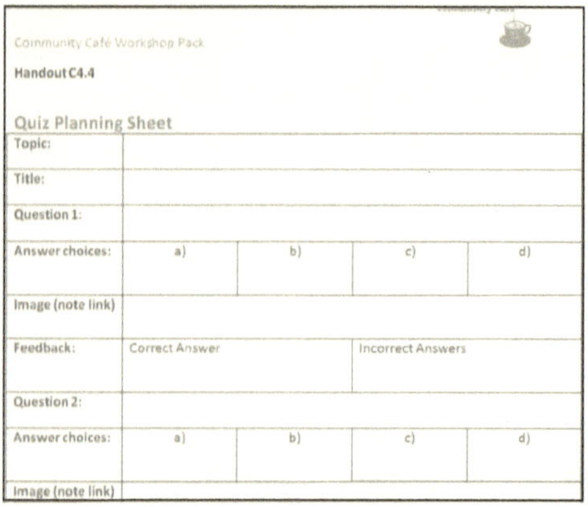

Figure 6. An online quiz for Punjabi produced as part of the workshop on creating online exercises http://languagebox.ac.uk/1778/

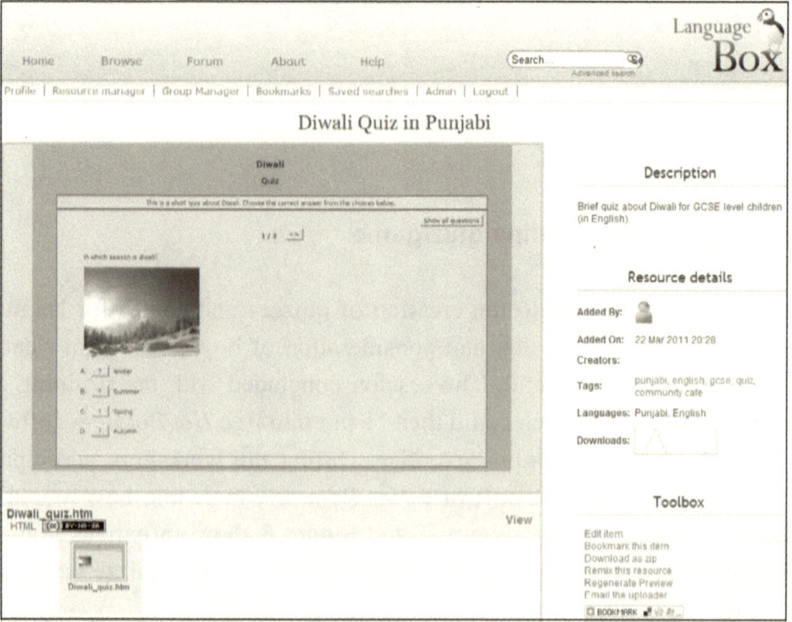

Figure 7 illustrates how all of the Community Café workshop activities could be combined into one interactive activity if participants had or learnt additional IT skills. This Hungarian resource includes 2 audio recordings and several online *Hot Potatoes* quizzes.

Figure 7.   A Hungarian resource which has combined many of the workshop activities into one interactive learning object http://languagebox.ac.uk/1733/

5.   Conclusion

The impact of this short project on the community-based language teachers who took part was significant. They acquired new technical skills, made new contacts with colleagues, reflected on their teaching methods and resources, and learnt more about using the internet effectively to find resources and to publish their own work. The City Council officer who runs the network noted that: "*tutors are already applying some of the things they have learnt in the classroom, and this has made a big difference to teaching quality*". He felt that the project had "*opened a new door for them [the tutors]*". This demonstrates that creating and publishing open educational resources within a social, community setting has the potential to be a vehicle for the development and enhancement of professional skills, particularly for a group marginalised from mainstream education.

The social, collegiate aspects of open practice-sharing were important in this process, both online (via LanguageBox): "*I have found the LanguageBox to be very useful as inspiration for my own lesson planning because I can get ideas from other teachers' lesson plans...*" and offline: "*Each teacher has different issues so it is interesting to hear different experiences. I have got some teaching ideas from other colleagues during café meetings*". The benefits and challenges of sharing open resources amongst an identified community group is one aspect of open educational practice and sits alongside institutional and national initiatives in OEP and OERs. For example, within the UK, research work continues in this area at the Open University, with language teachers using the LORO repository, and at the University of Southampton, with general humanities practitioners using the HumBox repository.

OEP offers a flexible, low-cost means to share resources, share practice and increase the pool of teaching materials for community-based language teachers. These activities are much needed and valued by community-based teachers, as shown by the number of downloads of project resources. Our short project revealed that tutors have great levels of enthusiasm for professional development and for open working, but it takes time to embed, absorb and act on new knowledge, and community-based teachers need continuing support and encouragement to help them access and build on ideas and experiences which may be commonplace to those in mainstream educational sectors.

Useful Links

The entire Community Café workshop pack detailing including all facilitator/ teachers' notes, participant handouts and templates, plus instructions for setting up your own community café can be found at: http://languagebox.ac.uk/1846/

A reusable Language Game Dice was produced by the project as an open resource. This OER is accompanied by teachers' notes and is available at: http://languagebox.ac.uk/1835/

Journal article about the project:

Borthwick, K., & Dickens, A. (2013). The Community Café: creating and sharing open educational resources with community-based language teachers. *Journal of e-Learning and Knowledge Society, 9*(1), 73-83. Retrieved from http://www.je-lks.org/ojs/index. php?journal=Je-LKS_EN&page=article&op=view&path%5B%5D=803

CILT, The National Centre for Languages: http://www.cilt.org.uk/home.aspx

JISC: http://www.jisc.ac.uk/

JISC Community Café Project reports: http://www.jisc.ac.uk/whatwedo/programmes/ digitisation/communitycontent/communitycafe.aspx

Languages Open Resources Online: http://loro.open.ac.uk

Project blog: http://communitylanguages.wordpress.com/

The HumBox: http://humbox.ac.uk/

The LanguageBox: http://languagebox.ac.uk/

9 The "Onstream" Project: Collaboration between Higher Education Teachers of Russian and Teachers of Russian in Mainstream and Supplementary Schools

Terry King[1]

Abstract

This case study describes how the problem of the isolation of teachers of Russian in supplementary (Saturday) schools in London was addressed by organising collaboration between them and teachers in a mainstream secondary school and a university. The aim was for them to share resources and pedagogical approaches. The project began with a meeting for identification of common needs and goals. A space in a Virtual Learning Environment (*Moodle*) was set up and subsequent activity was via an on-line discussion forum for exchanging ideas and a resource bank for sharing materials. Early on, the supplementary teachers visited the mainstream school to observe lessons. The ensuing resource bank was substantial; four short films of lessons in each sector, twenty items of teaching materials, two PowerPoints by teachers for classroom use and seven by their students on study topics. In their first venture into on-line Open Educational Resources, the team found the development of a culture of sharing among teachers faces many obstacles: differences in the context of the production and use of the created materials and in styles of pedagogy, the problem of non-take-up of resources and the psycho-sociological factors inherent in sharing with strangers. Yet, on the positive side, everyone recognised the benefits of sharing.

Keywords: collaboration, supplementary schools, cross-sector, Russian, OER.

1. UCL, London, UK; terry.king@ucl.ac.uk

How to cite this chapter: King, T. (2013). The "Onstream" Project: Collaboration between Higher Education Teachers of Russian and Teachers of Russian in Mainstream and Supplementary Schools. In A. Beaven, A. Comas-Quinn, & B. Sawhill (Eds), *Case Studies of Openness in the Language Classroom* (pp. 110-120). © Research-publishing.net.

1. Context: London, the multilingual city

At least 300 languages are spoken in London's mainstream state schools. All of the world's major languages are represented. Over 40 languages are each spoken by more than 1,000 pupils[1]. Some of these, currently called "community" languages, are taught in mainstream schools but most are taught in supplementary schools, i.e. small schools with their own teachers running outside school hours, in the evenings, on Saturdays, or on Sundays. A directory of schools in London, compiled by the 'Our Languages' project lists 283 supplementary and 43 mainstream schools which teach a range of community languages from Albanian to Yoruba. Many of these supplementary schools are part of a larger organisation dedicated to preserving the culture associated with the language.

Previous work on the ATLAS Olympics competition based in University College London (UCL), for secondary and supplementary schools in London, showed that language teachers in both sectors often desired to know more about ways in which the target language was taught in the other sector.

2. Intended outcomes

In September 2010, the author and colleagues in UCL were successful in gaining funding from Links into Languages, London, a government-financed initiative, to work with teachers of Russian in supplementary schools.

They had broadly three aims:

- to address the perceived isolation of teachers in different sectors and the desire of some supplementary school teachers to learn how to teach to the examinations set for mainstream learners;

---

1. Research conducted by the Department of Quantitative Social Science at the Institute of Education, London, based on data obtained from the Annual School Census of 2008 http://repec.ioe.ac.uk/REPEc/pdf/qsswp1012.pdf

- to create Open Educational Resources (OERs) useful to all sectors and to discuss their use;

- to improve the quality of the learning experience for students in both sectors.

3.   Nuts and bolts

3.1.   Recruiting

Focussing on Russian, the team recruited participants from three sectors:

- four supplementary schools for Russian in different areas of London (Bexley, Greenwich, Newham and Kingston);

- a mainstream London secondary school with a flourishing, highly successful, Russian Department of three teachers, with a year 10 class of twenty, a year 11 class of twenty studying for GCSE, a year 12 class of ten taking AS level and a year 13 class of eight taking A level[1];

- higher education: two teachers of Russian from UCL and a second year undergraduate class of twelve were involved.

The outcome was to involve ten teachers working with eighty pupils in total, sharing materials and ideas.

3.2.   Setting up

In September 2010, the team organised a workshop attended by seven teachers of Russian from the four supplementary schools, two teachers from the mainstream

---

1. GCSE is the exam taken in the last year of compulsory education at age 16; AS level is an exam taken in a chosen subject at the age 17 and A level is a continuation of AS with an exam taken in the year prior to entry to university at age 18.

school and one from the Higher Education Institutions (HEI). Prior to the meeting, participants identified problems and successful methods. Suggestions were made for likely areas to focus on.

Some supplementary students with Russian as their home language had little skill in reading or writing and needed help on how to prepare for GCSE and AS/A level exams. Under the new specifications, students needed help with writing their Creative, Discursive and Research-Based Essays - a problem shared by mainstream pupils. After a discussion of common needs, sharing knowledge of resources and pedagogical approaches and identifying specific agreed goals, a project plan was agreed and drawn up.

The pedagogic principle underpinning the project was that linguistic competence is developed when students are engaged through creative activity and have a sense of authentic communication, i.e. involving real situations and audiences. So it was agreed that the project would run in tandem with the CrossRoads2 project which provides undergraduates as e-mentors for school students in a password-protected, teacher-monitored environment (King, 2010). The virtual learning environment (VLE) used was *Moodle*. Each undergraduate student was paired with two students.

4.   In practice

4.1.   Using the VLE

The same *Moodle* site employed for the student e-mentoring was used for the *OnStream* project. The teachers were to use the Discussion Forum facility to communicate with each other and to contribute to a resource bank.

A large number of files from the mainstream school on the teaching content for A level and GCSE classes was uploaded, along with lesson plans and advice on conducting orals. Further items were uploaded by the supplementary school teachers.

4.2.   Classroom observation

It became clear from the teachers' Discussion Forum that OERs needed to be seen in the context of their use. So the supplementary school teachers were invited to observe three lessons (with years 10, 11 and 12) at the mainstream school.

The event was most successful as feedback showed. One supplementary school teacher said:

> It was a great experience to see Russian language to be taught a different way other than done in our supplementary school.

A discussion in the Forum on the different circumstances in supplementary schools followed. As a result more teaching materials were put up on the project website by all three sectors as well as material pointing out the differences between mainstream and supplementary teaching and requests for information. Another supplementary school teacher wrote:

> It will be interesting to know how do you give grammer [sic] topics and how do you choose an order of grammer [sic] introduction or criteria of importance. What children have to cover (from grammer [sic] point of view) at the end of year 10, for example.

At a meeting after the lesson the future direction of the project was planned. At the suggestion of the supplementary school teachers we expanded the scope of the project to include teaching methods as well as sharing materials. It was agreed to make a film of classes in all three sectors as a record of some of the differences.

4.3.   Filming classes

Accordingly in late December 2011 a film was made of a year 12 grammar lesson at the mainstream school and a link to it was put up on the project web site. In January, a film of a first year undergraduate lesson at university, also on grammar, was made. In March the third film was made in a supplementary school, on the topic of reading and literature. The three films clearly highlighted the contextual differences between the three sectors. The obvious ones are:

a) University class: small, motivated. Teaching in English.

b) State school: classes large and mixed in ability and motivation but of the same age. Teaching in English. Well resourced.

c) Saturday school: classes small and mixed in age, ability and motivation. Teaching in Russian.

4.4.   A competition for students

To involve the students creatively a competition was organised for all participating students to create materials, with vouchers for prizes. There were three sections – one for each of the levels –, GCSE, A and undergraduate. The students were asked to create a PowerPoint or word document on a topic suitable for the level at which they were studying and relevant to topics on the syllabus. These were:

- for GCSE: Russian customs and/or traditions, Russian celebration days;

- for AS/A level: Popular culture. e.g. An aspect of Youth culture, Popular Music, Leisure, Sport or Tourism;

- for undergraduates at university: an aspect of Russian "high culture" (e.g. a writer, composer, artist or an area, e.g. opera, ballet) or a topic from Russian history or current affairs.

4.5.   Student involvement in creating materials

The competition produced some excellent entries on topics ranging from the poet Anna Akhmatova and International Women's Day. Below is a slide from a PowerPoint on Russian popular music, written by an AS level student.

Figure 1. A page from a school student's PowerPoint on popular Russian music

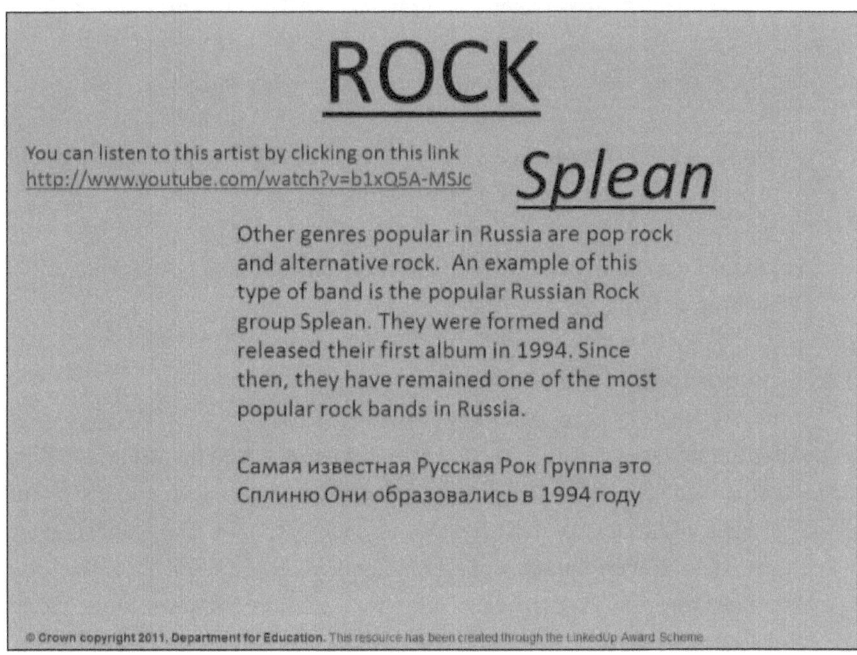

A selection of the materials created in the project can be seen on the Links into Languages website.

5. Conclusion

The aims were achieved, commensurately with the time and resources available.

In terms of the learners, reading the exchanges of the pairs of students in the discussion forum and judging by the enthusiasm of those who entered the competition, it is clear that some students were helped with their motivation. There were only a few cases of targeted support helping performance. Improvements in performance take a much longer time to evaluate.

As for the teachers, all those participating had access to the created resources and most expressed, at some time, their satisfaction with them. They all had exposure to a wider range of activities and practices. It would take more time to evaluate whether they were able to develop pedagogical skills as a result.

At the initial meeting, the supplementary school teachers were pleased to be included in the project, valuing the opportunity to collaborate with mainstream teachers. In the subsequent lesson observation, their immediate response was of great interest in the methods and resources of the mainstream teachers. One would hope that it contributed to a sense of belonging to a community of diverse practice.

As regards further supplementary and mainstream collaboration, this is an important aspect worth pursuing. Many UK schools, especially in London, possess a greatly under-used resource – the wide range of linguistic abilities of some school students. More should be done to bring those outside the mainstream into it. In this respect the *Onstream* project was, as far as the author knows, a first attempt to encourage collaboration between the mainstream and supplementary sectors. As a pilot it encountered successes and difficulties which future developers might like to consider.

5.1.   Successes

The project succeeded where it was able to:

- use students from all three sectors in mutually helpful activities in creating materials for each other;

- use demonstration lessons where possible so that the resources could be seen in context;

- use the specialist knowledge and expertise of the teachers whose first language is Russian;

- use the mainstream teachers' knowledge of and experience in teaching to UK exam syllabuses.

5.2.   Some difficulties

In our first venture into OER, it was found that the development of a culture of sharing among teachers faces many obstacles. One such obstacle was the differing context of the production and use of the created materials. At the initial meeting, it was felt that the participants had much in common and mutual help was possible. However, in the discussion forum, the supplementary teachers established that they worked in a very different context to the others. They were part-timers, teaching in the target language to small classes, mixed in age and with varying knowledge of that language.

Another obstacle was the different pedagogical styles of the teachers involved. The videos and observed lessons showed a variety of approaches, teacher-centred and pupil-centred. The resources ranged from the open-ended (e.g. web links with suggestions on their use or original writing for re-use) to the closed (e.g. worksheets for completion by the students). Worksheets and information sheets predominated, possibly because they are easier to share. There is a danger with OER that the easiest format for sharing might become the dominant mode for unimaginative teaching. For one teacher, grammar teaching is a matter of informing students of the rules and exceptions, exemplified in our resource bank by the sheets of grammatical tables. His students are passive receptors of information. Other teachers would want their students to be actively involved. One video shows a class being given some examples from which to deduce for themselves the patterns of grammar. Each approach produces different resources and methodology. One would hope that uploading resources for either would lead to a discussion about the effectiveness of each. Supplementary teachers are keen, sometimes untrained, volunteers, first language speakers giving up time at week-ends to teach the target language. Not all of them had the skill in English or the time to contribute to discussions on pedagogy.

The non-take-up of resources was a further obstacle. The short time-scale of the *Onstream* project did not allow a thorough investigation of the subsequent use of the uploaded resources. Creating a resource reflects the creator's own take on teaching. Ownership remains critical when the materials are offered to others. Resources alone are not enough; their quality and the way they are used matters.

Additionally, the psycho-sociological factors should also be taken into consideration. There are particularly sensitive areas when sharing with strangers. This would be true in a cohesive group but it is even more challenging for practitioners from a different range of circumstances. Some of the contributors to the forum were defensive and hesitant, others over-assertive. It takes time for a positive group dynamic to evolve.

A final obstacle was the limited use of the Teachers' Discussion Forum. In retrospect it would have been better to apply a lesson learned from the student mentoring – i.e. an open Discussion Forum is not the best way to develop involvement. Such a Forum tends to be dominated by one or two people with little participation by the others. With the students the best organisation was to use very small groups or even pairs. Maybe the same applies to teachers too.

5.3.   Future developments

On the positive side, everyone recognised the benefits of sharing. The work is on-going. A public web site has been set up to make the resources available to anyone. It is hoped that the idea might be taken up by teachers of other major languages taught in London schools and at London universities, such as Arabic, Bengali, Hindi, Polish, Portuguese, Punjabi, Turkish and Urdu. Certainly, London, as a major competitor in trading in the global economy, needs to recognise and capitalise on the rich linguistic diversity of all of its schools. OERs created, shared and discussed with reference to their context, in both mainstream and supplementary schools, would surely help to achieve this aim.

References

King, J. T. (2010). The CrossCall Project. In S. Guth & F. Helm (Eds), *Telecollaboration 2.0* (pp. 437-450). Bern: Peter Lang.

Useful links

ATLAS Olympics competition: http://www.ucl.ac.uk/atlas

'Our Languages' project: http://www.ourlanguages.org.uk/

Resources from the *Onstream Project*: http://www.linksintolanguages.ac.uk/resources/2589

The public site describing the e-mentoring work is http://www.ucl.ac.uk/crosscall

10 Learning to Share and Sharing to Learn – Professional Development of Language Teachers in HE to Foster Open Educational Practices

Annette Duensing[1], Matilde Gallardo[2] and Sarah Heiser[3]

Abstract

This case study presents the staff-development perspective of the 'Collaborative Writing and Peer Review Project' developed at the Department of Languages, at the Open University, UK, between November 2011 and March 2012. The project was set up to promote the professional development of teachers through collaborative writing and peer review, encouraging open educational practices (OEP) and by extension the production and publication of teaching resources in an open repository. As teacher developers working in a blended environment, the authors facilitate opportunities for sharing and developing good practice as part of a broad staff development programme to help teachers understand and integrate innovative approaches into their practice. Participants in this project brought with them a range of experiences as practitioners from their work with language students both at and outside the University. This case study focuses on the professional development aspect of this initiative. It presents the different aspects of the process and analyses teachers' involvement with social online tools and the impact on teaching practice of engaging with the process of collaboration.

Keywords: higher education, professional development, online collaboration, OEP, sharing, peer review.

---

1. Department of Languages, The Open University in the East of England, UK; a.duensing@open.ac.uk

2. Department of Languages, The Open University in the South East, UK; m.gallardo@open.ac.uk

3. Department of Languages, The Open University in London, UK; sarah.heiser@open.ac.uk

How to cite this chapter: Duensing, A., Gallardo, M., & Heiser, S. (2013). Learning to Share and Sharing to Learn – Professional Development of Language Teachers in HE to Foster Open Educational Practices. In A. Beaven, A. Comas-Quinn, & B. Sawhill (Eds), *Case Studies of Openness in the Language Classroom* (pp. 121-133). © Research-publishing.net.

1. Context: Staff development for language teachers in open learning

This case study presents the staff-development perspective of the 'Collaborative Writing and Peer Review Project' developed at the Department of Languages, Faculty of Education and Language Studies (FELS), at the Open University (OU), UK, between November 2011 and March 2012. The Department specialises in Supported Open Learning offering degree modules in English, Spanish, French, German, Italian, Welsh & Chinese (most of them from beginners to advanced). Students are geographically dispersed and study independently using mixed media teaching materials. They are supported by locally based part-time teachers through assignment feedback, email and forum contact, and online and face-to-face tutorials. The Department currently has more than 300 part-time teachers who are line-managed in teams by Staff Tutors (here referred to as regional academic managers). Regional academic managers are locally based academics whose roles include, among others, responsibility for the continuing professional development of their teams of language teachers.

In the current ever-changing socio-educational context, the professional development of language teachers evolves around the idea of lifelong learning and the need for ongoing familiarisation with new ideas and skills. However, as Seely Brown and Adler (2008) have demonstrated, the process of learning and developing expertise is associated with reflection and participation in the field, in other words, to "acculturating into a community of practice" (p. 19). When working in a technology heavy open learning context (see above) this will be a "virtual community of practice" (Seely Brown & Adler, 2008, p. 18) making use of professional academic development by technology. As teacher developers working with a diverse group of part-time practitioners in a blended environment, regional academic managers facilitate opportunities for sharing and developing good practice as part of a broad staff development programme which incorporates aspects of the blended learning tools to help teachers understand and integrate innovative approaches into their practice. The multimodal environment in which the University-supported open distance learning takes place already enables teachers to acquire technical expertise and pedagogical understanding of a variety of digital tools including online social networking tools, as well as to developing positive attitudes towards sharing and discussing experiences of practice. Examples of this include recent staff development projects on Peer Observation of Teaching, Differentiation and more recently Dyslexia and Modern Language Learning, which have involved a strong element of collaboration and building on the work of others using synchronous and asynchronous online tools.

The project was one of nine funded under the University's Scholarship of and for Teaching strategy as it relates to two of its key thematic areas, enhancing teaching and learning with new technologies and developing professional identities and practice expertise, which underpin the Faculty priorities for its programmes of study.

2. Intended outcomes: Encouraging collaboration in teaching material production

The project was set up to promote the professional development of teachers through collaborative writing and peer review, encouraging open educational practices (OEP) and by extension the production of content for open publication and reuse. All teachers are likely to have different strengths and weaknesses and varying levels of prior experience, and benefit from discussions with colleagues. Therefore, regional academic managers at the Open University support their teams of part-time teachers by providing sample resources, thus helping the teachers in designing their own effective tutorial activities to work with students in the OU's Supported Open Learning system. For this purpose an online resource bank (LORO) is made available.

This initiative presented an opportunity to encourage teachers to make sharing, peer reviewing and reusing of teaching resources part of their routine working practices. Prior to the project, most teachers' engagement with the online resource bank was predominantly receptive: it consisted of downloading teaching materials for their particular student group or browsing resources for inspiration. Only some teachers engaged more fully in this online community of practice, by uploading new or reversioned materials and even fewer interacted with others through comment, offering praise or suggestions on uploaded resources. The project was set up to give teachers an opportunity to engage with the repository more fully during a defined period of time, in which support was available and engagement of peers with similar motivation was guaranteed.

The University's geographical spread across the UK at times limits the amount of regular contact between members of staff working in different locations. For the teachers in particular this can lead to demotivation, as they work part-time and from home, and may feel cut off from their teaching team. They might expect to deal with teaching issues in isolation or conversely become overly dependent on line manager support. The project therefore aimed to motivate teachers by providing opportunities for collaborative contact and working with peers, and to form subgroups for future joint working. The collaboration also enabled the different staff groupings to gain insight into each other's perspective, and to improve their use of the technologies available for teaching and collaborative working, through employing them practically in a dedicated task.

It was hoped that the project might lead to a targeted enhancement of the material provision, as teachers would identify and fill gaps they perceived in the existing collection. Furthermore, project participants might henceforth become champions of open practice: they might guide others in the use of the repository and lead by example in uploading of and commenting on materials, i.e. they would knit together the community of practice. An important aspect was for participants to engage with issues relevant to OER material development such as reusing materials or ideas developed by others.

Finally, the project was an impetus for all participants to engage in scholarship by reflecting on their own professional practice. Working with OER principles provided a supportive context, in which they could build on the existing scholarship by academic colleagues and an established network for dissemination.

3.   Nuts and bolts: Participants, technical tools and project schedule

The Department of Languages uses LORO, Languages Open Resources Online, to address the need to support its teachers as producers of tutorial activities for online teaching. LORO is an online repository of open educational resources (OERs) and was developed with JISC funding in 2010 to aid storing, sharing and accessing language teaching resources provided by the OU.

The project team brought together three regional academic managers and three members of the LORO development team who were course developers and coordinators. It worked in close co-operation with the twelve participating teachers. This triangle united a range of expertise, given the diversity of roles and backgrounds. The attributes sought in the teachers were the ability to deliver good, communicative language tutorials, having a firm understanding of diverse student need and inclusivity, having previous experience of creating imaginative and effective materials, familiarity with the LORO repository and, ideally, experience of collaborative work. The teachers, drawn from a diversity of languages, brought with them a range of experiences as practitioners from their work with language students both at and outside the Open University.

A designated online environment on the institutions' Moodle environment was set up for the project. The tools afforded were asynchronous forums, wikis and an online synchronous web-conferencing 'room'. The forum was provided for discussion and for communication between the project team and participants, for example, setting schedules and giving information. As the sub teams of participants formed, it was envisaged they would set up strands for their collaborative work. The wiki was set up for collaborative material development. The online 'room' (Elluminate) was available for synchronous meetings, either by the whole group as part of scheduled input sessions or the autonomous subgroups to discuss their joint work.

Table 1 below shows the schedule of tasks and steps planned by the project team.

Table 1. Collaborative writing and peer review project schedule

Stage	Dateline	Action	Tools
Preparation	Over a 4-month-period prior to launch	Project team meetings to design and plan	Synchronous and asynchronous conferencing
Recruitment	Month 1 (1-hour-session)	Invitation to all OU language teachers Briefing meeting for all interested teachers Finalising participant list	Advert (LORO Newsletter - October 2011 - LORO), email Online room Project mailbox
Training and discussion	Month 2 (2-hour-session)	Project launch (participants and project team). Session introduced participants to LORO functionality, the concept and history of OER and OEP and explored aspects around collaboration and peer review	Online room
	Month 3 (2-hour-session)	Presentation and discussion of tools for collaboration, using third party material and copyright issues, and creative commons licenses. Group formation and planning discussion	Online room
Group work	Month 3 to 4 (2-week-period)	Collaborative writing and peer review; participants from each group create • one new resource • one resource based on reuse/reversioning	Synchronous and asynchronous conferencing. Email
Progress meeting	Month 4 (2-hour-session)	Presentation and discussion of resources; discussion of collaborative writing and peer review	Online room
Completion	Month 4 to 5 (2-week-period)	Finalising and uploading of resources, peer commenting	LORO
Dissemination	Month 5 and beyond	Opportunities for participants to present at staff development events, championing LORO, OER and OEP	LORO, online room, face-to-face in various locations

Scheduled sessions were designed to be interactive and discussion-based so as to harness the participants' experience, to demonstrate the possibilities and strengths of peer support and to address the actual needs of teachers in this particular work context. Task outcome guidelines for subgroup formation and working were deliberately left flexible to allow for a good degree of autonomy.

4. In practice: How the plans were applied and received

Overall the project ran as scheduled in the plan set out in Table 1. Some variation occurred in the working of the subgroups, largely due to their choice of online tools.

Through forum postings and synchronous online discussions, participants formed four groups for joint work with those of similar interests (Table 2).

Table 2. Group and resources produced

Group:	Resources produced:
English for Academic Purposes	A case study about a bookshop with activities
Jing embedded video descriptions	Learning to use the tool and making resources
Intermediate Italian	Pronunciation, tongue twisters, description of an apartment activity
Cross languages	Materials in different languages for reversioning, differentiation and extension activities

During the group work phase participants had to organize their own schedule and work more independently. Here they mostly chose tools they were familiar with such as email for communication. Whereas it was quick and easy to use, this meant the work was not visible on the forums, and one participant, inadvertently left off one email, missed part of her group's work.

Time constraints meant that participants had no or few synchronous subgroup meetings. If at all, they used their own teaching rooms with preference over the project's room, access to which was less familiar to them.

Participants only used new tools if they afforded clear benefits. The wiki was the only tool new to some of the participants, and only one group used it to design their materials. One group introduced another tool, 'Jing', for short video recordings, explored how to use it, and used it to create materials.

The project produced 19 useful teaching resources which can be found on the LORO website by searching for the 'collaborative writing' tag. Two are illustrated in Figure 1 and Figure 2.

Figure 1.   Teaching resource in LORO created during the project[1]

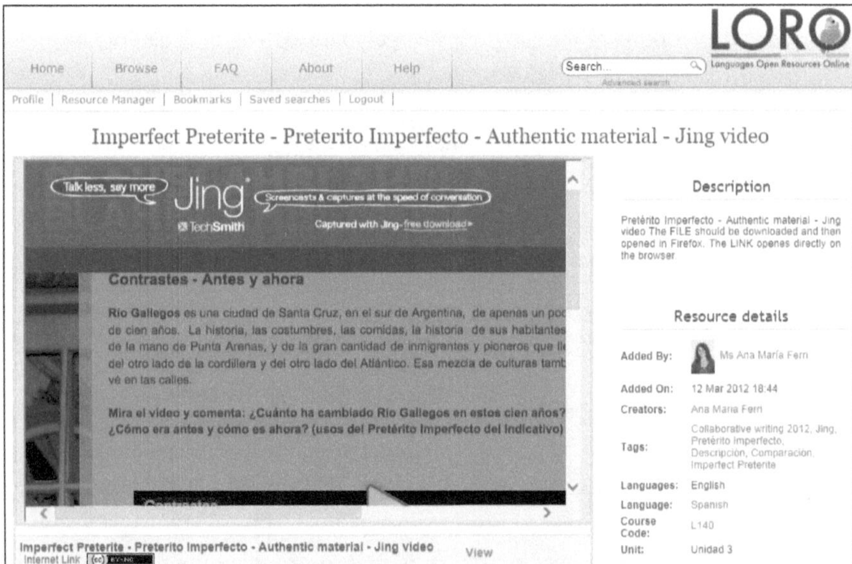

In a final evaluation of the intended outcomes, eleven participant questionnaires were returned. When asked if they would use the materials produced in the project, 8/11 participants reported they would definitely use the materials they had produced themselves, 4/11 would use the materials produced by their group and 2/11 would use those created by other groups.

---

1. Jing activity: http://loro.open.ac.uk/2851/

Figure 2.   A beginners' French activity adapted for German[1]

The experience of writing collaboratively with new people was described in the final evaluative questionnaire as "highly motivating". Another participant commented,

---

1. French activity: http://loro.open.ac.uk/535; German activity: http://loro.open.ac.uk/2951/.

"I think we had a shared underlying understanding of what constitutes effective teaching and were open to each other's ideas."

Participants were particularly positive about the helpfulness of peer support available through working in groups. When asked about giving and receiving comments 8/11 agreed the comments were valuable and none disagreed; one reported feeling uneasy having their work commented on, but 8/11 said they did not. Nevertheless, they were clearly aware that peer review has to be provided sensitively, as 6/11 said they felt uneasy making the comments, while only 2/11 did not. Figure 3 illustrates how tutors supported each other through constructive and tactful feedback.

Figure 3.   An example of developing peer evaluation
             and comment in LORO

Participant 1, 02 Jun 2012 18:25
This is a very good idea, [name]. What sort of questions would you ask? For example:
'Quante finestre ci sono?' 'Quale stanza non ha finestre?'

Participant 2, 02 Jun 2012 17:27
This is a wonderful listening activity. How about adding some questions? This would
help the students notice some of the language you used e.g. 'la cucina è abitabile'

Participant 3, 28 Apr 2012 23:09
I think this is a really good idea of how to exploit the course materials further by adding
a new dimension to them. Thanks for a great idea, [name].

While participants experienced the time constraints involved in collaboration, overall they felt that this was worth it. However, when asked if working collaboratively took more time than working individually opinions were split. 6/11 agreed and 4/11 disagreed, while 5/11 thought it would save time in the long run and 3/11 did not.

The majority of participants reported having benefitted from the enthusiasm generated by the working in groups and giving and receiving comments. One participant concluded,

"It was a very interesting and useful exercise. It encouraged me to work collaboratively and I appreciated the benefit of it. I have certainly learnt different things such as how to use new tools in order to make my material more interesting and interactive. Furthermore, since I took part in this project I started re-using and adapting existing materials and it is saving me lot [sic] of time. Finally the project encouraged me to share my work and ideas with other [sic]: I liked to have feedback on my work before publishing it online (I thought it was very encouraging and reassuring), I have also been inspired from the work of other people."

5.   Conclusion

Following the principles of Open Educational Resources and Open Educational Practices as defined by Wiley (2007) among others, this case study illustrates how a staff development initiative for teachers of Modern Foreign Languages in Higher Education represents a good example of integrating OEP and OER into teachers' professional practice. The benefits of working collaboratively using social networking tools and publishing resources through open repositories have been indicated by participants in the project. By engaging with innovative pedagogical practices they found the process of collaboration a motivating and enriching learning experience which also gave them the opportunity to reflect on their attitudes towards and perceptions of ownership and open access. The process was underpinned by the use and reuse of individual teaching contributions to adapt them to the needs of learners as identified by the extensive teaching experience of participants. Thus some of the comments and feedback express the idea that materials produced collaboratively become "part of a community" and can be regarded "more as a proposal or a suggestion" rather than the creation of one individual. The impact of this initiative goes beyond improving teaching practice and it is reflected in the quality of the student experience as they benefit from the use of better resources and more confident teachers.

The full integration of LORO in the professional practice of Open University language teachers will be a long-term achievement which requires further work to raise awareness and build skills amongst users, as well as regular monitoring among practitioners. However staff developers feel that the experience of this project has taken participating teachers to a level of "champions" and has offered great encouragement to teachers to be involved in staff development events and to play a key role in promoting collaborative OEP to the wider community at the OU and beyond. As a result, many participating teachers have already given presentations and run workshops for their peers at regional and national level events while some others have engaged in scholarship.

This case study not only illustrates the process of engaging practitioners with the production of open educational resources but, more significantly, we have provided a practical example of successful and innovative open educational practices in the context of Supported Open Learning, which has the potential to be replicated and adapted to a variety of settings. The project further demonstrates the potential of social networking tools to develop teachers' digital literacies required by the changing role of the practitioner in teaching languages in blended contexts.

Acknowledgements. The authors would like to express their gratitude to all participants of the project, in particular Ana Maria Ferri and Caroline Rowan-Olive whose resources are featured in figures 1 and 2 respectively, and Anna Comas-Quinn, Tita Beaven and Christine Pleines, who are central academic members of the Department of Languages on the project team.

Useful links

JING: http://www.techsmith.com/tutorial-jing-embed-content-using-screencastcom.html

JISC: http://www.jisc.ac.uk/whatwedo/programmes/infl1/sue2/loro

LORO: http://loro.open.ac.uk/

LORO newsletter: http://loro.open.ac.uk/2637/

Supported Open Learning: http://www.open.ac.uk/about/main/the-ou-explained/teaching-and-learning-the-ou

References

Seely Brown, J., & Adler, R. P. (2008). Minds on Fire: The Long Tail and Learning 2.0. *EDUCAUSE Review, 43*(1), 16-32. Retrieved from http://www.educause.edu/ero/article/minds-fire-open-education-long-tail-and-learning-20

Wiley, D. (2007). Iterating towards Openness. Retrieved from http://opencontent.org/blog/archives/355

Collaborative Learning & Student-generated Content

11 Transnational Online Discussions to Foster Open Practices

Klaus-Dieter Rossade[1]

Abstract

This case study reports on the outcomes of asynchronous task forums in an advanced language and culture course in the Department of Languages at the Open University (OU). In these task forums, distance learners have the opportunity to discuss a variety of topics that relate to the themes of the course and are closely embedded within the materials. Learners share their understanding and opinions immediately after they have worked through a particular resource or section in the materials. The examples and quotations are based on contributions from the 2011 cohort. One example, a forum discussion about what learners make of the term *Heimat* (homeland), revealed a high level of interaction between participants which was based on authentic personal experiences and required little teaching input. Even learners with lower than required levels of German contributed regularly and used the forums to try out target language discourse in the protected space of the course. The principles and examples presented here point to a successful open educational practice which is transferrable and could be turned into user-generated open educational resources themselves. The case study also discusses some of the technical and structural nuts and bolts of such task-based forums.

Keywords: open educational practice, distance education, language learning, asynchronous task forums, transnational language learning, self-organisation of learners.

---

1. The Open University, UK; Klaus-Dieter.Rossade@open.ac.uk

1.   Context

The OU, with over 200,000 learners annually, is the largest distance education provider in the UK. The course *L313 Variationen Advanced German* (from now on referred to as L313) is the last of four German courses, which take learners from beginners to advanced language proficiency (level A1 to C1 of the Common European Framework of Reference for Languages, CEFR). L313 is a 31 week language and culture course and attracts between 120-140 mature learners (the largest segment is 35-55 years). Learners study a blended mix of books, audio, video and web activities on a Moodle Virtual Learning Environment (VLE), all of which are carefully scripted to match their needs.

Generally, distance learners study the materials independently at a place and time of their choice, often alongside work and family commitments. Learners are allocated to what is called a tutor group at the Open University and the teacher (or tutor) marks assignments, gives feedback and provides general study support. The teacher runs face-to-face and online synchronous conferencing tutorials where learners meet and study with their peers. Learners can also communicate via two asynchronous forums, one for their tutor group and one for the whole course cohort. The task forums analysed here are additional to these standard offers and voluntary. The assignments are ultimately the only compulsory element on L313 and time-poor distance learners tend to prioritise compulsory course components and consider carefully whether to interact in task forums or not.

Figure 1 below shows the first of six blocks in the course on the topic of geography and political structures of German speaking countries (*Landschaftliche Vielfalt und politische Strukturen*). Task forums are in week one, two and three and in these, learners discuss their favourite places or regions in German speaking countries, places they would like to visit, how these compare with places or regions in their own countries, what homeland (*Heimat*) means to them and what they think of Wilhelmshaven, a city in north west Germany which they have just studied in the course. On the left pane of the screen are the general discussion spaces (student forum and tutor group forum).

Figure 1.   L313 Variationen VLE
showing the first five weeks of study.

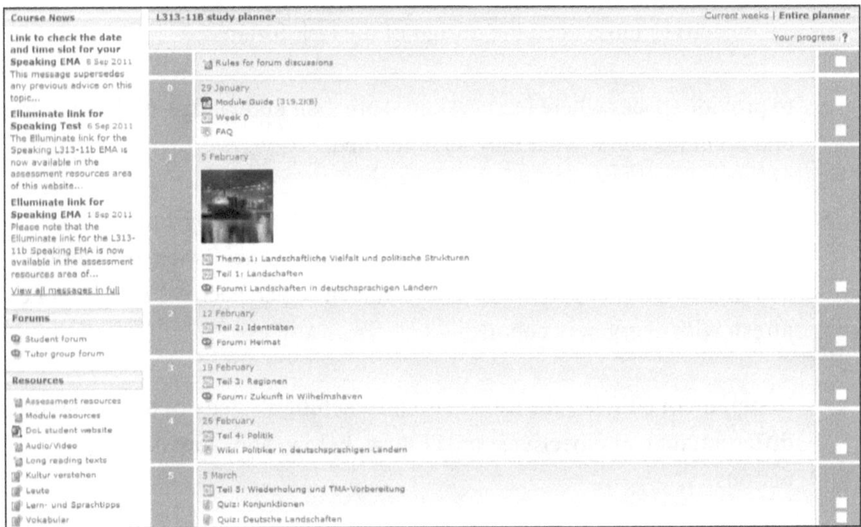

The course takes learners through the advanced level (CEFR C1), but the actual learners' ability can range from upper-intermediate (B2) to native or near native (C2), a result of the university's open entry policy: learners receive advice about the level required to study the course but ultimately the decision remains theirs: linguistically weaker B2 learners often sign on hoping to catch up over time whereas stronger learners may study for the content or just to get the credits for a degree in Language Studies.

Linguistically stronger learners are often foreign learners who have lived or live temporarily or permanently in German speaking countries, or German speaking foreigners on the British Isles, or perhaps second generation heritage speakers in the UK: the shades and permutations of learners' backstories are infinite and enrich any discussion within the course. Most learners have studied other courses before with the institution and are therefore experienced distance language learners.

2.   Intended outcomes

Four key objectives influenced the design of the task forums:

- to provide spaces where learners can share their knowledge, understanding and opinions about what they have learned;

- to encourage intercultural comparison and reflection by linking tasks to topics and questions that aim to utilise the learners' rich backgrounds and intercultural experiences. These authentic perspectives are generated afresh with every new cohort;

- to support or enhance the transnational teaching strategy by strengthening differentiated perspectives on culture below and above the level of nations;

- to evaluate the level of self-organisation of the group, and, by extension, the teaching resource that is needed to support pedagogically meaningful forums which add value to the learner experience.

The first three objectives took Karen Risager's (2007) proposals for a transnational language and culture pedagogy as a starting point and the forums emulate to some degree her concept of the transnational classroom for distance learners.

Language development and language practice were also expected outcomes but as an additional benefit only. No error correction is offered and learners are not required to communicate in German (weaker learners are encouraged to start in English initially to boost their confidence). The course developers also anticipated socio-affective benefits as distance learning can be a solitary experience, but again, these benefits are not central and are also covered by other forums.

Selection of communication tool: Simple text forums were considered the appropriate tool for the objectives outlined above. Communicating via text forums is comparatively easy and learners are used to these from their tutor group interactions. With asynchronous forums, learners stay in control of their time and the extent to which they contribute. Such forums allow learners to study other contributions in detail, to reflect, to draft and to revise their own text before they publish it. Forums were also very easy to integrate into the learning materials. This leaves learners just one click away from the (inter)action and offers the choice of pull i.e. accessing the forum to read messages, or push i.e. subscribing to forum message delivery to their email accounts.

3.   Nuts and bolts: Integration of forums

The forums are located on the L313 Moodle VLE. The task forum design on L313 is learning object orientated: learners enter discreet discussion spaces for each topic. The discussion is part of a series of linked activities related to just one topic (see Figure 3), not an activity for which learners have to leave the context of the learning resource. The embedded discussion is more akin to the comments sections attached to, for example, online newspaper articles where readers can immediately comment on what they have just read and share their views instantaneously. This learning *object* metaphor is different from a general discussion or social *space* metaphor, such as the tutor group forums in the course, which learners enter when they want to socialise and then create or participate in threads for a variety of purposes.

Figure 2 shows such a discreet space for a discussion about the increasing use of English words in German. Learners worked through authentic resources and performed some basic web searches before they contributed to the discussion. Most responded to the first strand *Denglish, gut oder schlecht* (mash-up of

German-English, good or bad) but several other strands were started, often without a clear rationale and perhaps by accident. However, the discussion remains bounded to the topical space with the task at the top and the subscription facility at the bottom.

Figure 2.   Forum about the increasing use of English in the German language

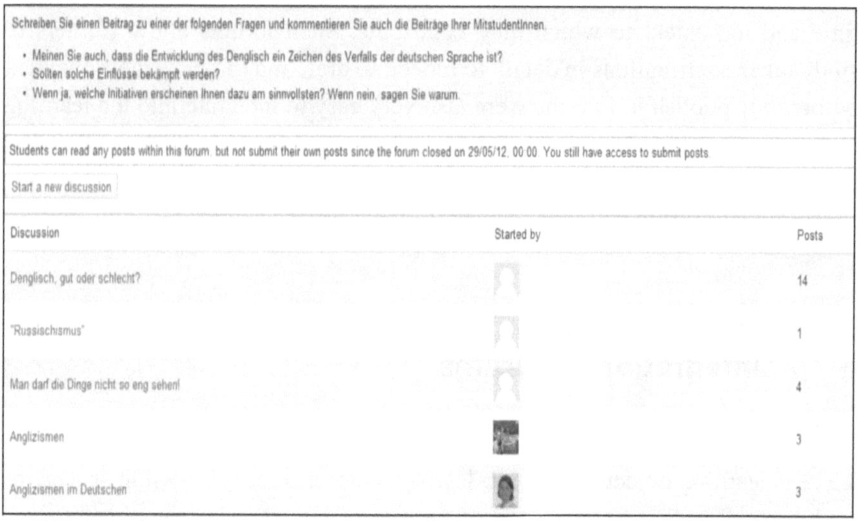

The tasks are often adapted from reflection notes which are spread across the printed and online materials and invite learners to consider particular aspects further (*Zum Weiterdenken*). The forums thus transform individual reflection activities into interactive group processes. This transformation is supported by tasks which are seamlessly embedded in the learning path: a click through to a forum discussion does not feel any different from the click to a third party website.

All topics and tasks offer opportunities for intercultural comparison, ranging from tasks that require little or no preparation (e.g. describe your favourite place or region in a target language country or the country of origin, what not to joke about?, what do you think about dual nationality?) to those that rely on considerable pre-task work (e.g. homeland, emigration, asylum in Germany and Europe).

The moderation of the forums was shared in 2011 by a team of teachers. As the fourth objective was about how the group organises its discussion, each moderator was asked to intervene as little as possible, but was invited to contribute at times to the discussion 'as participants' reflecting on their personal intercultural interpretations, attitudes and experiences.

4.   In practice

Figure 3 illustrates a sequence of activities that deals with the concept of homeland, a concept that remains heavily charged within German speaking cultures. Having worked through several learning resources about homeland, learners are asked, in activity 1.2.10, to explore a quote ("Only those who know the past, know the present") in light of their impressions of some local history museum websites that they were asked to visit. They were asked for example to define the term "local history museum" and their mission today, and perhaps relate personal experiences with such museums. In activity 1.2.11, learners then go to the forum *Heimat* and discuss questions from the previous activity with other learners. The more limited questions about local history museums expand to learners' general attitude towards *Heimat* and learners reflect as a group on all they have learned so far as well as their own personal experiences. Then, in activity 1.2.12, learners return to the individual distance learning mode and work through a cued speaking activity on the topic.

The forum on homeland has been popular every year since the course started in 2010. In 2011, 22 learners from a total of 128 at course start (17.2%) and 101 sitting the exams (21.8%) contributed around 8900 words to this forum, which also included two short moderator posts (150 words). Each of the 51 posts on the topic averaged about 175 words, each learner writing 387 words on average. It seems not unjustified to describe this exchange as very lively and the following summary aims to give a brief flavour of the exchanges.

Figure 3.   Forum on *Heimat* (Homeland)
embedded within distance learning tasks

1.2.10 Heimatmuseen

Sie lernen jetzt einige Heimatmuseen kennen. Auf der Webseite des Heimatmuseums Obersdorf steht:

„Nur wer die Vergangenheit kennt, kennt die Gegenwart."

Lesen Sie die Fragen und sammeln Sie Informationen dazu auf den Webseiten der Heimatmuseen. Klicken Sie entweder auf die Internetadressen oder suchen Sie nach Webseiten von anderen Heimatmuseen, die Sie vielleicht kennen oder interessieren.

- Stimmen Sie der Aussage des Zitates zu?
- Welchen Beitrag können Heimatmuseen dabei leisten?
- Wie könnte man den Begriff „Heimatmuseum" definieren?
- Welche Aufgaben haben Heimatmuseen heute?
- Waren Sie schon einmal in einem Heimatmuseum? Was hat Ihnen gefallen? Was hat Ihnen nicht gefallen?
- Was halten Sie persönlich von Heimatmuseen?

  Heimatmuseum Oberstdorf

  Heimatmuseum Treptow und Köpenick

  Heimatmuseum Falkensee

  Heimatmuseum Berchtesgaden

1.2.11 Forum Heimat

Gehen Sie in das Forum „Heimat" und diskutieren Sie mit anderen Kursteilnehmern und Kursteilnehmerinnen, was Sie herausgefunden haben. Schreiben Sie auch, was Sie persönlich über Heimatmuseen und den Begriff Heimat denken.

Schreiben Sie mindestens einen Beitrag im Forum und kommentieren Sie einen anderen. Es ist nicht schlimm, wenn Ihr Beitrag sprachlich nicht ganz korrekt ist. Hier geht es darum, mit anderen Teilnehmern und Teilnehmerinnen Informationen und Meinungen auszutauschen.

Forum „Heimat"

- Stimmen Sie der Aussage des Zitates zu?
- Welchen Beitrag können Heimatmuseen dabei leisten?
- Wie könnte man den Begriff „Heimatmuseum" definieren?
- Welche Aufgaben haben Heimatmuseen heute?
- Waren Sie schon einmal in einem Heimatmuseum? Was hat Ihnen gefallen? Was hat Ihnen nicht gefallen?
- Was halten Sie persönlich von Heimatmuseen?

Antwort zeigen

1.2.12 Über Heimat sprechen

Sie nehmen jetzt an einem Gespräch mit einem Experten zum Thema Heimat teil. Teil A führt Sie Schritt-für-Schritt durch den Dialog, in Teil B können Sie in Echtzeit sprechen.

A

Nehmen Sie jetzt Ihre Fragen auf (Aufnehmen). Lesen Sie zur Vorbereitung jeweils die Antwort zu Ihrer Frage in Klammern. Vergleichen Sie Ihre Version (Abspielen) mit dem Modellvorschlag (Modell). Hören Sie zum Schluss die Antwort Ihres Gesprächspartners (Hören).

(Guten Tag. Ja, ich habe mich schon seit langem mit diesem Thema befasst und einige Gedanken dazu aufs Papier gebracht.)

Many contributions proposed a variety of definitions from geographical locations that people felt attached to, to emotional perspectives such as "where my heart is", where one felt secure in the past, of a life people remember well and happily. However, concerns were voiced, too, for example from a Swiss national (MPZ-C2+)[1], who explained the Swiss citizenship concept of *Bürgerort* (citizen rights tied to a local community, not the nation). He called *Heimat* a delicate, patriotic, nationalistic and even segregationist concept, while an English emigrant in Germany (FRLW-C2) had issues with the concept "'*Heimat*' without a plural". A third learner (MAH-C1) reminded the group of minorities and their need or yearning for a homeland and, on balance, considered emotional attachments to a *Heimat* entirely acceptable and apolitical, but conceded that it had been misused by the Nazis. This was followed by more than 30 posts within eight days on multiple strands, until one learner (FAC-C1) took on the task to provide a summary of the discussion so far. This learner, born and raised in an Eastern European country, now lives in the UK as a dual national, holds a joint English degree and has thirty years of teaching experience in modern languages. She delivered a substantial blog post (1,272 words) which observed academic conventions, organized the discussion around the principle of "homeland – security versus freedom", quoted and paraphrased key contributions from other learners or course resources, and extended the discussion with references to further relevant resources such as Edgar Reitz's (1984) TV-series *Heimat*. Taking all these contributions together, the notion of *Heimat* becomes a place that one can call home for a variety of reasons. These need no longer be framed and shaped by nations exclusively but can operate at a transnational level, whether in sub-national geographic categories or extra-national emotional or ideological categories.

The homeland forum demonstrates the collective power of reasoning and the sensitive navigation of a complex concept that a group discussion can deliver, where participants contribute knowledge, experiences and opinions from various geographical, socio-cultural and educational backgrounds. Together they raise the sensitivity of the whole learner cohort, including those learners who do not contribute but simply read the posts, in the case of the homeland forum at a ratio of one active contributor to three read-only participants.

---

1. The person reference includes <gender><id><CEFR-Level>.

5.   Conclusion

This case study revealed a high level of independent learner engagement with the task and self-organisation of the group discussions that required only low levels of teacher intervention. It could therefore be seen as a good example for open educational practice even if, in this case, it took place in a password protected space of some 120-140 learners. It is open to learners' personal and intercultural experiences which they can share, and it is openly supportive of all learners irrespective of their backgrounds and variations in language proficiency. The *Heimat* forum demonstrated how a comparatively simple question can lead to complex outcomes which deliver on all four objectives mentioned in Section 2. This performance was replicated in other task based forums on the course, albeit at different scales and intensities, depending on the nature of the task and the topical preferences of the learners. There was no questionnaire that elicited directly learners' attitudes towards these forums, but based on the analysis of all contributions one might like to suggest five key elements that may have helped to make these forums vibrant and informative:

- Authenticity: Learners narrated very personal episodes and emotions and this was frequently acknowledged by others who seemed to be encouraged to share their stories in turn. The summary above masks the richness of experiences and often the rich language with which learners recounted their individual perspectives and reflections. As they considered, confirmed and corroborated each other's experiences in the course of the discussion, they also outlined collective culturally bound attitudes without necessarily ossifying these into national stereotypes.

- Contextualisation: Forums are tightly embedded in the flow of learning activities. The timeliness and one-click access to a discussion may support active participation when the thoughts and reflections about a topic are still fresh. In addition, learners are also likely to be influenced by previous discussions: the *"Heimat"* forum is preceded by a forum on learners' most favourite places and regions which may have primed them to think in sub-national categories. Consider by contrast the potential priming effect if a previous forum had asked them about typical stereotypes about Germans.

- Purpose: Learners were told that the task forums are not primarily for language learning, but for sharing knowledge, understanding and ideas. This was underlined by the invitation to write in English if need be, though no learner took up this offer. On the contrary, many learners who initially had not quite reached the required level of linguistic ability to contribute with ease, continued in German. Rather than switching to English, they appear to have accepted the challenge and used the forum space for experimenting with their language skills.

- Self-organisation: Learners were aware that the forum was moderated, but also realised that teacher interventions were rare. This may have helped participants to take responsibility for their discussion and contribute in ways that are natural to them, e.g. by providing summaries or additional links to resources from time to time.

- Object orientation: Forums are linked to learning objects and not merely a thread amongst others in a generic discussion space, where older discussions are displaced by newer threads. The task forums keep all threads together and can easily be revisited later for example when quotes or ideas are needed in assignments.

The forums are protected spaces for learners to practice discourse before they enter the open world of web forums which have become a standard feature on most content platforms across the internet. The forums in this case study may be seen as the 'sandpits' where learners try and test their readiness to join the world on open online communication. And just like the discussion strands following YouTube or news channel resources are becoming sources of information themselves, the discussions presented here could turn into user-generated content for future foreign language learners.

References

Reitz, E. (1984). *Heimat: A chronicle of Germany*. Germany: Edgar Reitz Film GmbH.

Risager, K. (2007). *Language and Culture Pedagogy. From a National to a Transnational Paradigm*. Clevedon: Multilingual Matters.

12 A Case Study into Learner Engagement in the Production of OERs within an Online Language Environment

María Dolores Iglesias Mora[1] and David Elvis Leeming[2]

Abstract

This case study demonstrates examples of how open practices and resources can be used to effectively engage language learners in the learning process. The case focuses on a small group of Spanish Open University learners (Beginners Spanish programme - L194 Portales) that began their language course in October 2012. The case shows a successful way of using the forums as a 'portal' for distance learners to interact, create, share and cooperate in the Virtual Learning Environments, and argues how the method employed enhances the learning experience. It also illustrates how the learners actively used the target language in their interactions which then gave them confidence to build upon their language skills. Furthermore, the case study offers the reader a model to embed into their own practice, and explains the organisational considerations behind the results should practitioners choose to replicate the methodology. It concludes by postulating that OERs can offer a real opportunity to create a strong sense of learner autonomy by encouraging the learners to become engaged in the activity of creating their own authentic materials.

Keywords: open educational resources, OERs, teaching forums, online feedback, authentic materials, interactive learning, learning experience, autonomy, collaboration.

1. Open University, UK; m.d.iglesias-mora@open.ac.uk

2. University of Central Lancashire, UK; deleeming1@uclan.ac.uk

How to cite this chapter: Iglesias Mora, M. D., & Leeming , D. E. (2013). A Case Study into Learner Engagement in the Production of OERs within an Online Language Environment. In A. Beaven, A. Comas-Quinn, & B. Sawhill (Eds), *Case Studies of Openness in the Language Classroom* (pp. 149-161). © Research-publishing.net.

1.   Context

Open Educational Resources (OERs) have come to the fore in recent years, as the use of technology within education has flourished. Many authors, such as Hanna and Wood (2011) have observed the pedagogical benefits of the individualisation and personalisation of online learning materials. Clearly many within the educational field are acutely aware of their potential, especially as cost effective teaching resources.

Whilst the advantages seem obvious, could there be a missing link in this innovation? It is the authors' strong belief that the learner experience should be at the heart of all that we undertake as educators; indeed their professional practice is based upon this conviction. Hence a sharing community of teachers and learners, in their opinion, is the perfect arena to take this belief to another level.

It has often been observed that language learners feel most engaged when they are afforded the opportunity to focus on what is important to them, for example, the chance to talk about their family or hobbies; it gives them a sense of ownership and familiarity. It has also been observed in their teaching by the authors that there is often a desire to use authentic materials by both learners and teachers.

The authors' experiences have shown time and again the usefulness of this form of pedagogical engagement. They felt that their enthusiasm could be translated into how learners engage with the curriculum by producing, sharing and using their own authentic materials. That is, by transferring to the learners the ethos that sharing OERs is a good and productive practice, the learners would eventually understand that cooperative productive learning can make a real difference to their learning experience.

Therefore, the main purpose of the following case study will be to investigate the potential for turning leaners' production in the target language into OERs. The authors intend to, firstly, show and review the results from this relatively new angle and come up with some conclusions and suggestions for future work.

2. Intended outcomes

Many within the field of education have recognised the benefits of fostering a culture of sharing work that can then be adapted and developed according to the needs of a particular teacher and group of learners. In recent years the authors have been involved in the creation and adaptation of OERs that have been uploaded and 'published openly' in LORO (Language Open Resources Online). This experience has been extremely useful, and therefore Ms Iglesias Mora (an Open University teacher) decided to experiment with this further by also engaging her students in the production of these materials.

Initially, the main goal of the project was to encourage learners to produce their own learning resources in order to consolidate their language learning. An additional goal was also to evaluate to what extent this involvement affects retention and progression of learners. At the same time, from the pedagogical point of view, the intention was to examine how this could help foster learners' autonomy and motivation as well as build a social, collaborative feeling amongst the learners. The project also explored other possible potentials of teaching forums beyond their use as simply discussion boards.

Overall, the project was initiated to increase awareness, both for teachers and learners of the benefits of incorporating Open Educational Resources into materials design and teaching by generating language learning resources and publishing them openly so that other teachers and learners could reuse and adapt them to their particular needs. Moreover, the intention was to model a collaborative learning environment (using teaching forums) as a way to introduce learners to the roles and responsibilities that learners will need to adopt should they choose to produce OERs.

3. Nuts and bolts: Organisation

The teacher felt that the best way of fostering this collaboration among the learners was to initially use the group forum, a teaching forum used only by a particular group of learners and their teacher. This was used as a 'portal' to enable learners to exchange and create their own electronic materials in the way of podcasts, short video/photo documentaries, PowerPoint presentations, and Word Documents related to the themes that learners dealt with in their course. First, the teacher posted an introductory message giving details of her expectations regarding the use of the forum and encouraging learners to participate actively. Once learners in the group got to know each other and the sense of community started to take shape, she then posted one task that gave the learners the opportunity to produce some learning material as well as practising and consolidating the language they had learnt.

Figure 1.   A resource uploaded to LORO

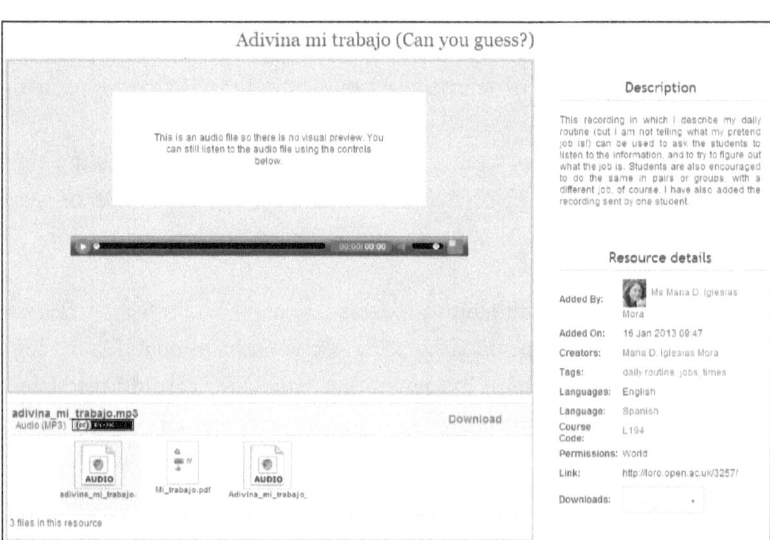

The teacher's role during this time was, first of all, to encourage and facilitate the exchange of ideas, as well as guiding in the creation of these materials. By doing this, the teacher was attempting to promote a common ground where sharing is a productive way in which learning can happen. She then edited the material sent by the learners by correcting any possible mistakes in the final version as well as giving feedback to the learners on the language they had used.

Finally, with the learners' permission, the teacher agreed to upload the materials onto LORO, the repository of language teaching materials based at the Department of Languages at The Open University. This repository can be used by anyone, although it is mainly aimed at language teaching professionals. Figure 1 above illustrates how one of these resources has been shared openly and how it has been downloaded by other users.

4.   In practice

In this section we present a few examples of tasks that were posted in the teaching forum, and how open educational resources were developed from them.

4.1.   Task 1
"Mi familia" (My family)

Figure 2 below shows one of the tasks posted by the teacher. In this message, the teacher is clearly initiating the creation of a collaborative learning resource by sending her own audio file with a description of her family and a family photograph. To make it a bit more challenging, some of the information in the recording does not match the photo. The idea is that the learners can listen to the recording and try to figure out what is the information that does not match the photo. Then, they are encouraged to reply by discussing the teacher's material in order to consolidate their own learning.

This is also an 'excuse' to encourage the learners to replicate, create, share and discuss their own audio files as learning resources amongst the rest of the participants of the forum.

Figure 3 below shows one of the replies. In this case, the learner has chosen to post a written paragraph (Word document) together with her own family photo. She explains that she has added four pieces of information about her family that do not match the photo.

Figure 2.   Initial posting of the task by the teacher

Figure 3.   Reply from a learner to the original teacher post

The teacher edited part of the original document to improve the presentation of the resource and to give some constructive feedback to the individual learner, which would also be of benefit to the whole group. She felt it was not necessary to correct all the mistakes the learner had made at this stage because she did not want the learner to be put off by an excessive number of corrections. Further feedback was given via email.

Following this initial posting, other learners replied to the teacher and the learner in Figure 3, pointing out the information that did not match the family photo:

Reply by RS 23 Nov 2012, 12:11: *Hola a todos. ¡Muy bien! Helen.*

En el photo <u>lleves</u> un vestido negro, Will y James <u>lleven</u> vaqueros azules y tu madre <u>lleve</u> un abrigo negro. Yo mandaré un photo pronto. Un saludo

One could already see the interaction among the learners is starting to take shape.

The teacher posts other messages to give feedback to each individual learner regarding the target language used in their replies as follows:

MI (23 Nov 2012, 21:28): *Hola Ellen. Well done! La descripción de tu familia es muy buena. Qué simpáticos!*

Great effort. I have checked and edited a few words for you...hope you don't mind me doing it. If you prefer me to do it by email, let me know. Un saludo

ED (26 Nov 2012, 11:53): *Thank you Maria, that was very helpful and i can see where i went wrong! Ellen*

This shows how the learner is already starting to see the benefits of this collaborative work and the fact that by sharing she can also learn. Then, RS posts a recording with his description and several photos of his family (Figure 4).

Figure 4.   Reply to the original teacher post and the other learner post

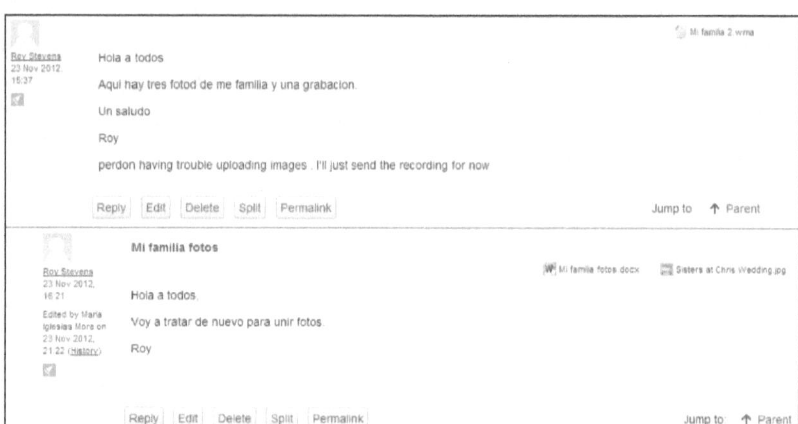

By doing this, he is attempting to follow the teacher's material and to personalise it in order to be shared with the rest of the group. The learner is already adapting and reusing the material that the teacher and his classmate have previously posted even though he may not be overtly aware of this. The teacher's job at this stage is limited to making sure she acknowledges the learners' contributions and keeping the momentum in order to facilitate the forwarding of the discussion. She only participates to encourage contribution from the other learners in the group as well as giving feedback and editing the postings whenever is necessary.

The text above shows how the interaction among two of the learners in the group is beginning to show its benefits. Their roles are starting to become more proactive as they engage in the adaptation and sharing of their materials. That is to say, they take the initiative to comment on each others' materials as well as using these to benefit their own learning. We feel at this stage the learners could probably post their ideas as a way of practising the target language but they do not necessarily understand they are starting to develop new skills to share and collaborate openly.

It is important that the teacher introduce them to this new role in a progressive way in order to make them aware of the benefits of moving from being just passive recipients to becoming active participants in the learning process that will culminate in the sharing and creation of OERs. This highlights that teacher facilitation, guidance and support are essential and needed throughout the whole process.

We can see that throughout this process, the learners take the initiative to generate their own materials in order to be posted in the teaching forum, whilst the teacher only participates to encourage contributions from the other learners in the group as well as giving feedback and editing the postings whenever is necessary.

With the learners' permission, these resources could be polished and uploaded to LORO for other teachers and learners to use or reuse. By guiding learners to eventually have their materials published as OERs we are also giving them an incentive to increase their motivation and consolidate their own learning by being more focused on producing quality work that they know would be shared with the community. This certainly seemed to be an incentive for the learners to spend the extra time not only to produce materials, but materials they would be happy for others to view and comment on or add to.

As an extra benefit to the learner, we also believe this process helps instil a feeling of ownership in the learners. The learners have fed back that they felt a feeling of 'pride' by sharing their work with others, and that collaboration gives them a sense of being part of a wider community rather than an isolated learner. Arguably the skills gained from experiences like this go beyond the language and deepen their skill set in other ways from communicating ideas, presenting their work online, to critically and analytically thinking and reflecting on the comments they make and the comments made about their work.

4.2. Task 2
"Adivina mi trabajo" (Guess my job)

Figure 5, Figure 6 and Figure 7 illustrate another example of a forum task that leads to the creation of an OER to be shared outside the course.

Figure 5.   Initial posting of the task by the teacher

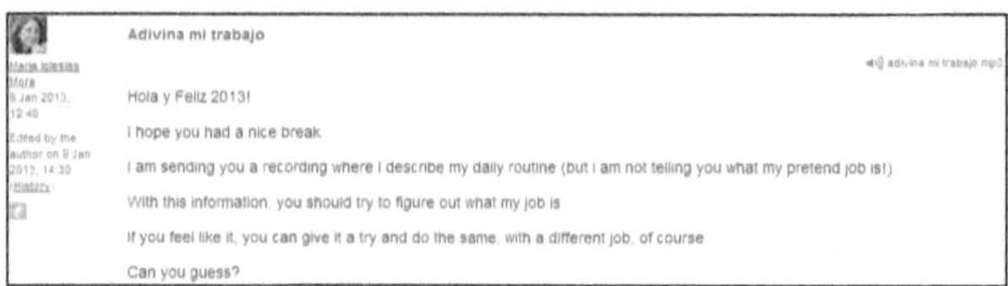

Figure 6.   A learner's reply to the teacher posting

Figure 7.   Learner's posting with audio resource
and teacher's feedback audio file

The teacher finally asks for permission to publish the material onto LORO:

> MI:(4 Feb 2013, 10:24) *Hola Roy. I was wondering if you could record your message again bearing in mind my feedback.*
>
> *If possible, and with your permission, I would like to incorporate and publish your work together with my recording in LORO. I think it's very good. Please, let me know what you think. Un saludo. P.S Any guesses about Roy's "mystery" job? Would anyone like to give it a try?*

The above sequence shows one particular example of a learning resource that was successfully created by one of the learners and then uploaded onto LORO so that other teachers and learners can access it. The material includes audio files produced by both the teacher and the learner.

However, we consider it is equally crucial to introduce the learners to the OER 'environment' in the first instance so that they can have a better understanding of the implications of what would happen to their recordings, photos and writings. We think this could also have an impact on their motivation, since the learners know the material is going to be eventually published and shared openly with other teachers and learners.

5.   Conclusion

In conclusion, this case study has emphasised how OERs can not only offer opportunities for learners to use their creativity in the target language, but also to produce materials that suit their interests and that are based on their personal experiences. It has also shown how the teacher's facilitation, guidance and support are needed throughout the whole process. Although the project is still ongoing, from the authors' preliminary observations one could suggest that learners seem to have gained more confidence within the very short period of time that they have been engaged in the process and have increased their collaborations and shared initiatives in the teaching forum.

At the time this case study was written, the majority of learners in this group were still reluctant to take part in the forum and to share their ideas. This is most likely due to it being a new concept, which the learners will need to be introduced to progressively. We cannot expect the learners to grasp the concept of collaborating openly straightaway and, we believe, the degree of learners' involvement depends very much on the extent to which the teacher would model this collaborative learning environment (using the group forum in this particular case) in a positive way so that learners can see more clearly the benefits of sharing.

Given the predominance and relative importance society gives toward online social networks, this activity tries to encourage the formation of a sense of community amongst learners, who are otherwise working in isolation, at the same time that they are introduced to new roles and responsibilities they need to adopt when producing OERs in a collaborative learning environment.

If time had allowed, it would have been very interesting to have collected more in depth evidence from this fruitful experience and analysed those emails and postings from the teacher and the learners in more detail. It would also have been interesting to collect feedback about the process and results from the learners.

Nevertheless, what has been shown here are the possibilities of an open, learner-centred approach to motivate learners by offering a chance to develop learner autonomy and the sense of belonging to a shared community.

It is clear that the results are limited. However there are obvious possibilities, certainly for an online-based community. There is no doubt that this project could be easily re-purposed and tried out by practitioners in different teaching contexts and levels.

It would be very interesting to undertake the same project with Intermediate and Upper Intermediate learners of Spanish in order to compare and analyse the findings related to learners' interactions and collaboration in producing language resources. For this reason, in future, the authors' would like to carry out a comparative study to examine whether the level of language proficiency of learners influences the active participation in the teaching forum. They postulate that a greater linguistic ability would lead to greater participation as these learners would most likely feel more confident sharing and commenting on materials due to their higher linguistic proficiency. One could compare this to how we grow more comfortable with a language the more we understand and use it.

The authors' would also like to investigate to what extent the level of technical proficiency has an impact on the degree of sophistication of the design of the materials created by the learners. Would the use of the technical media, for example the advanced use of video diaries/journals offer more motivation for involvement than simply using text input? Of course the support of the teacher both from a linguistic and technical perspective would continue to be essential.

Acknowledgements. Many thanks to Miss Ellen Davies and Dr Roy Stevens, both Beginners' students of Spanish (L194) from October 2012. Their contributions have been invaluable both in the sessions they attended, their posts, and their collaboration for this case study.

References

Hanna, A., & Wood, D. (2011). Bridging the gap between OER initiative objectives and OER user needs in higher education. In G. Williams, P. Statham, N. Brown & B. Cleland (Eds.), *Changing Demands, Changing Directions* (pp. 539-551). Proceedings ascilite Hobart 2011. Retrieved from http://www.ascilite.org.au/conferences/hobart11/downloads/papers/Hanna-full.pdf

13 The OpenLIVES Project: Alternative Narratives of Pedagogical Achievement

Irina Nelson[1] and Alicia Pozo-Gutiérrez[2]

Abstract

This case study presents collaborative work undertaken as part of a project funded by JISC: OpenLIVES (Learning Insights from the Voices of Émigrés from Spain). The aim of this project was to develop Open Educational Resources based on a digital corpus of oral history interviews and archival material collected in the course of an earlier project that researched migrant life histories in contemporary Spain. This case study focuses on how the University of Southampton developed different types of pedagogical intervention which turned undergraduate students from passive consumers of received knowledge into active and reflective producers of educational material that was both central to their own learning and also relevant to a wider academic and non-academic audience. In describing these pedagogical interventions this case study presents a line of work developed at Southampton that not only forges independent and reflective language learners and future professionals but also widens participation and the transmission of knowledge beyond the academic community. Student engagement with open practice was key to these outcomes, and we believe that our experience at Southampton can offer a model of engagement which will be of interest to teachers of language and language area studies.

Keywords: open educational resources, students as producers, innovative teaching, learning approaches, Spanish area studies.

1. University of Southampton, Southampton, UK; irina.nelson@soton.ac.uk

2. University of Southampton, Southampton, UK; apg@soton.ac.uk

How to cite this chapter: Nelson, I., & Pozo-Gutiérrez, A. (2013). The OpenLIVES Project: Alternative Narratives of Pedagogical Achievement. In A. Beaven, A. Comas-Quinn, & B. Sawhill (Eds), *Case Studies of Openness in the Language Classroom* (pp. 162-175). © Research-publishing.net.

1.   Context

This case study presents collaborative work born out of a project funded by JISC which aimed at developing Open Educational Resources (OER) based on a digital corpus of oral history interviews and archival material. This material had been collected in the course of an earlier project that researched migrant life histories in contemporary Spain called "Tales of Return: The Memories and Experiences of Spanish Returnee Migrants from France and Great Britain (1950s-1990s)".

Led by the Centre for Languages, Linguistics and Area Studies (LLAS) at the University of Southampton (UK), the OpenLIVES project (Learning Insights from the Voices of Spanish Émigrés), brought together lecturers from Modern Languages Departments at the Universities of Southampton, Leeds and Portsmouth. These project partners used and adapted the corpus in different ways before embedding it in their Spanish curricula. This case study focusses specifically on the work done at the University of Southampton.

The different types of pedagogical interventions developed at the University of Southampton sought to transform undergraduate students from passive consumers of received 'knowledge' into active and reflective producers of educational material. The aim was that this material would become central to students' own learning, and at the same time relevant to the wider academic community and to a non-academic audience.

The development of Open Educational Resources involved undergraduate students of Spanish at beginner and advanced level (first years and finalists), and also final year students from a Spanish Area Studies module: 'Exiles, Migrants, Citizens: Narrating and Documenting Displacement in Contemporary Spain'. This particular module engages students in critical analysis of a variety of primary and secondary sources that document migration. These sources include personal testimonies, interviews, documentaries, migrant periodical publications and representations of migrants and exiles in various media.

2. Intended outcomes

Broadly speaking, the primary objective of the OpenLIVES project was to publish a set of existing research data and to create a set of open educational resources that tutors and students from the three participant institutions could use and reuse. Ultimately, we wanted to show that a corpus of research data collected for a specific project could be put into pedagogical use and be further developed and expanded by participants other than the original researchers for the benefit of a wider academic community. As part of this process, we sought to engage students across the three participant institutions in the creation of the learning materials, and to do so in a way that recreated a real professional environment marked by a spirit of true collaboration.

The project also sought to demonstrate that a single set of research data collected for a specific purpose and discipline can be used in a wide range of different ways within humanities and social science disciplines. We also wanted to contribute meaningfully to the current strategic objectives for Higher Education, such as employability, the enhancement of student learning and digital literacy.

In order to fulfil these objectives, Southampton fostered a "learn by doing" pedagogical approach that promotes the transferability of skills to the professional arena. In the course of the project, for instance, participant students displayed evidence of the successful development of skills in collaborative work related to a variety of relevant professional settings, for example, transcribing and translating material from audio and video interviews prior to dissemination and publication.

These learning processes are exemplified by a particular task that connected the work of Modern Language students from two of the participant universities. This task consisted of the planning of a follow-up interview with one of the original interviewees (a former evacuee child of the Spanish civil war) which was then filmed by staff and students at the University of Portsmouth. Students at Southampton then worked collaboratively to create subtitles for this video, thus transforming it into a learning resource and widening its appeal as a bilingual

OER. The final result is available in the open access repository Humbox under a Creative Commons license, which enables students and teachers from all over the world to continue to work with this material and develop it in new, creative ways (Figure 1).

Figure 1.   Open access repository Humbox showing some OERs from the OpenLIVES collection, which enables students and teachers from all over the world to reuse and recreate learning material in new creative ways

With regards to language learning specifically, the work done at Southampton aimed at developing tools for language acquisition by embedding the production and use of OERs into the language curriculum. An example of how this was done involved students with a very basic knowledge of the language (beginner level) working with authentic digitised material to analyse and reflect on the use of different past tenses in Spanish. The evidence of the students' involvement in this respect showed not only full understanding of the use of these verbal forms at the end of the task, but also made evident their ability to produce OERs for their peers in the form of Power Point presentations that became language learning and teaching materials (OERs).

The authors believe that through these pedagogical interventions developed at Southampton, we have encouraged our students to become independent and reflective language learners, as well as to develop some of the skills they will require in the future as professionals. At the same time, and given the nature of the materials we are working with – the life histories of people who witnessed key moments and processes in the histories of Spain, Britain and Europe (e.g. migrations, exile, wars, political transformations, dictatorship, democratisation, economic crisis) – our student community has contributed to widening participation and has fostered the transmission of knowledge beyond the academic community. In other words, our students have contributed to giving a voice to key protagonists of history from different generations, which can be heard beyond the University campus. Our student engagement with open practice is central to these outcomes, and our experience at Southampton has offered a model of engagement which will be of interest to other Modern Languages tutors and researchers from different disciplines.

3.   Nuts and bolts

The key driving principle behind the pedagogical approach of the OpenLIVES project was to blur what we saw as an unjustified boundary between the teaching of Language and Content units in the Modern Languages curriculum at Southampton. According to this division, Language units refer to the teaching of Spanish language alone, whereas Content units refer to the teaching of social, cultural and political aspects of the Spanish-speaking world. With this in mind, we did not necessarily wish to change existing practices at our institution but to establish bridges and to integrate Language and Content teaching to make it more meaningful for the students and to promote the transferability of practical and critical skills between the two.

We therefore worked from the language teaching and socio-historical perspective in order to foster in the students a critical approach to language use in society. At the same time, we wanted the students to critically explore the social and historical contexts of the different periods mentioned in the analysed testimonies. With this we promoted the critical analysis of language in use so that the students could explain the position that the speaker, as active agent in the historical processes, adopted within the social context that marked his/her life experiences. By exploring these contexts in the target language, we not only fostered an in-depth language analysis, but at the same time a critical approach to the understanding of the shifting historical experiences of Spanish society.

Our corpus of 24 interviews amongst Spanish economic migrants and former evacuees from the Spanish Civil War, as well as additional memorabilia, was digitalised and made available for open access in the digital Repository Humbox by the LLAS OpenLives team. Our students transformed some of these primary data into OERs using video-editing tools, subtitling tools, sound-editing tools (Windows Movie Maker and Audacity) and other teaching and learning materials produced in existing units. The resulting OERs would then work as learning-teaching resources that would be available for re-purposing as pedagogical material.

At Southampton, we used existing courses and curricular structures to foster the involvement of our students with the newly digitalised material. While critical assessment in the form of an essay had to be produced individually, other projects such as subtitling or grammatical analysis were developed in groups.

The digitalisation of the primary data was carried out by the Southampton-based LLAS team with funding provided by JISC to launch the OpenLIVES project. As well as the digitalisation and dissemination of a vast oral history corpus of testimonial material, the project also digitalised a great part of the contemporary documentation collected in the course of the interviews carried out in the original research project, such as written memoirs, photographs, press cuttings, drawings and artefacts (Figure 2).

Figure 2.   Benita Mendiola (first one from the right) with two other Spanish evacuees in the Soviet Union. Circa 1956

4.   In practice: The work of OpenLIVES

The work of OpenLIVES fostered collaborative work amongst lecturers and Spanish language teachers from the other participant institutions, Leeds and Portsmouth. Within Southampton, students' production of OERs was assessed as part of the formative assessment of both Language module and Content modules as discussed above.

The developments required for the involvement of our students as producers of OERs demanded the creation of specific tasks and mini projects that made us reflect and act on certain issues and deploy specific skills which we outline below:

- Engagement of our students not only in working with 'authentic' material but also in putting into practice 'authentic' professional skills such as transcribing, synopsis writing, applying linguistic analysis, editing, translating and subtitling. These tasks were successfully completed as practical skills were developed enhancing student motivation as they worked with real scenarios producing purposeful re-usable material (OERs);

- Engagement of the teachers and directors of the project in a wider discussion on the ethics of working with oral/life history testimonies and clearance and copyrights issues: this important question emerged when we felt that we needed to seek continued consent from informants that had previously given their testimonies in the context of a different research project, especially as OpenLIVES was going to make their interview material accessible online. Our students, as co-producers of their learning materials became aware of this vital dimension, signing their own consent forms prior to publishing their own OERs on line;

- The newly created OERs produced by students also included synopses of each digitalised interview produced by final-year students of Spanish at Southampton. The students acquired a new skill in the area of translation and were employed later after graduation as members of the LLAS team to work in a similar role;

- At Southampton we engaged the students from two different pedagogical perspectives: from the language learning perspective via their Language course modules, and from the Content unit perspective, via modules that dealt with socio-cultural and socio-political aspects of the Spanish-speaking world, which require skills such as critical thinking and analysis which are assessed in the form of essays written in English.

From the language learning perspective, the students were engaged through working with grammar at beginners' level. Their assigned task consisted of documenting the historical context and language use of an extract of an original interview of a Spanish refugee from the Spanish civil war, who was evacuated to the former Soviet Union. The students produced OERs in Power Point format using digital tools to edit voice and illustrate the language use examples they were presenting. This work is now in Humbox as an OER to inform other students about language use in a particular historical context in contemporary Spain. Our current student cohort of beginners' Spanish is using the material produced by the previous cohort to inform their production of new OERs to explore Spanish language use at basic level and to inform their contextualisation of the primary data. These activities promote the exploration of Spanish contemporary history by solving a language task (Figure 3).

Figure 3.   Slide from PowerPoint presentation produced by students to learn the simple and imperfect past tenses in Spanish using an audio extract from the life history testimony from Benita Mendiola, Spanish 'child' emigre to the Soviet Union who currently lives in Madrid, Spain

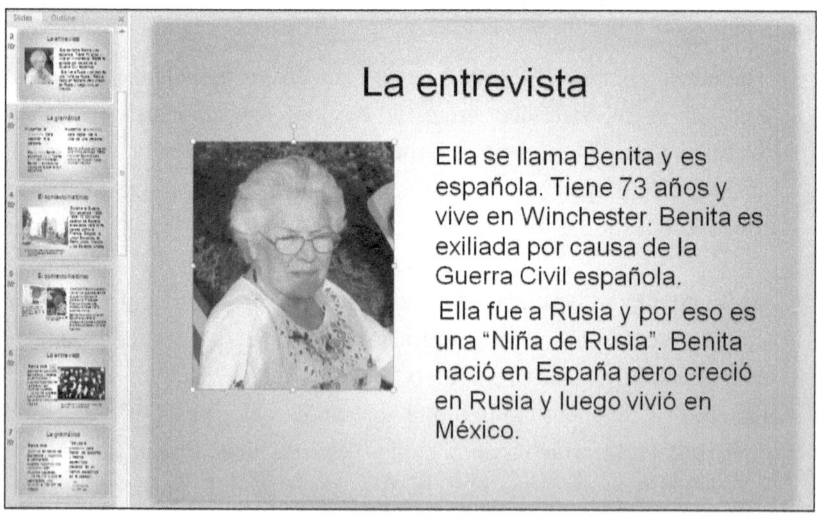

From the perspectives of both language acquisition and political history analysis, the students engaged in a subtitling project. The task demanded that they perform different roles within their group, which they distributed amongst

themselves mimicking how most Translation Companies are organised in the professional world. Part of the task involved learning the operational logic of a translation company. Thus, our students distributed amongst themselves their roles as: Transcribers, Translators, Proof-Readers and Editors.

The translation process required a critical analysis of the political, historical and social context in Spain during the years of the civil war and its aftermath. Their translation strategies depended on their linguistic proficiency as well as their critical historical knowledge of the period. In the course of their work, for instance, they encountered politically-charged words and terms that needed to be faithfully transmitted.

The technical process of the subtitling project required that the pragmatic meaning of the original message in Spanish was expressed in less than 75 characters in two lines per visual frame; however, meaningful semantic units could not be separated and this presented a challenge that was successfully overcome. A new sophisticated skill was thus successfully acquired by our students. The final product is of high professional standards and has been made available as an OER in Humbox (Figure 4).

In terms of new roles, we can say that overall, our participant students have developed new roles as producers of published OERs. By this we mean that they have become not only producers of their own learning materials, but also co-researchers and even contributors to current commemorative practices and events, where they themselves become witnesses of historical processes. For example, a group of students participated as volunteer helpers in the 75th Anniversary Commemoration of the arrival of nearly 4,000 Basque evacuee children to Southampton in 1937 which was held at the University of Southampton on 11-12 May 2012. By attending and working at this event, our students became social agents in their own right, and witnesses of a historical process that links the past with the present. Aware of this special role conferred to them by their active participation, they agreed to record their experience and interaction with the former evacuees in interviews carried out by Pedro García-Guirao, a PhD student at Southampton. These interviews, which document the impact of their engagement in this event in their own personas, as students, as members of the community and as researchers, are now a new OER that can be accessed at Humbox.

Figure 4.   Subtitled interview of Germinal, former evacuee child of the Spanish Civil War as a resource produced and transformed by students and currently accessible in Humbox

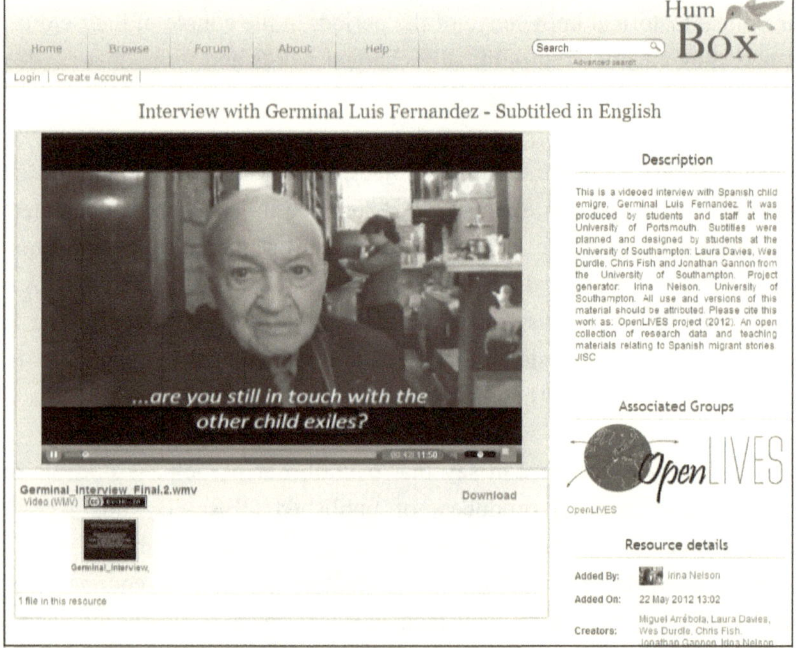

5.   Conclusion

OpenLives has generated alternative narratives of pedagogical engagement that challenge some academic assumptions in unexpected and perhaps necessary ways. First, the collaborative scope of the project surpassed all our expectations in terms of outputs and personal learning. Colleagues from the three partner universities used the corpus of testimonies in ways that we could not have envisaged when the material was first collected as raw 'data'. Building on the methodology of the initial project (Tales of Return) and on drawing an oral history research tradition well established in its Modern Languages Department, the team in Southampton developed learning tools that provide a model of research-led teaching and learning that puts migrant life histories at the core of both language and content courses. This transcends what some of us have regarded for some time as an unfounded subject division. Blurring the traditional boundaries of language and content curricula in this way challenges two long-held assumptions: 1) that language teaching has no significant content and 2) that content teaching should not prioritise language use.

Second, the engagement of students in the process of digitalisation and transformation of the data has been extraordinary in terms of level of commitment and quality of outputs. The idea of 'the student as producer' captivated the imagination of the team from the start. In an educational setting dominated by the mantra of 'employability' there is no better way to learn than by doing and engaging in authentic and relevant activities. Working together tutors and students have revitalised and disseminated the original material in creative and hopefully enduring ways.

A third benefit that can be extracted from the testimonial nature of the OpenLives project has to do with the very nature of oral history, empowering and revealing as it is of alternative historical interpretations. Being exposed to them has encouraged all participants to consider their own personal positioning (cultural, national, generational, political) within a wider global context where narratives of migration are part of a historical continuum.

Finally, the project has opened up our 'pedagogical minds' to the idea that open access can contribute significantly to the democratisation of learning and in doing so undermine what many academics in the UK see as the increasing commodification of education. Through dissemination under Creative Commons Licencing the testimonial corpus at the heart of OpenLives has become organic, subject to continuous development and enrichment by different constituencies of users which may include the protagonists of these migration stories and their descendants. The interdisciplinary dimension and the intergenerational dissemination scope of the OERs are key strengths that can be developed further. At present, lecturers, teachers and students in higher, secondary and further education, as well as the public at large, can use and learn from the material created. They can do so from the perspective of a multiplicity of disciplines (history, narratology, linguistics, sociology, film, politics…) and they can continue to develop it in unforeseeable ways, adapting it to ever changing social, migrational and educational contexts.

By digitalising and making accessible this material to the public we are finally being honest to the people who generously shared their life histories for the purpose of knowledge generation and transmission. Making the collaborative work ethic that underpins it sustainable in the long term is the next challenge.

Ackowledgments. We are grateful to the University of Southampton for the Adventures in Research grant that enabled Alicia Pozo-Gutiérrez, Scott Soo and Darren Paffey to gather the original data. We are thankful to JISC who provided funding that enabled the OpenLIVES project to transform the original data into Open Educational Resources. We are indebted to Kate Borthwick and Alison Dickens from LLAS for the management and coordination of this project. Finally, we thank Miguel Arrebola and his students from the University of Portsmouth for their inspirational collaboration and our Modern Languages students from the University of Southampton.

Resources

Audacity tutorial: http://audacity.sourceforge.net/manual-1.2/index.html
Windows Movie Maker tutorial: http://windows.microsoft.com/en-gb/windows-vista/getting-started-with-windows-movie-maker

Sources cited

Humbox. Retrieved from http://humbox.ac.uk/

Interview with Germinal Luis Fernandez – Subtitled in English. Humbox. Retrieved from http://humbox.ac.uk/3664/

JISC. Retrieved from http://www.jisc.ac.uk/whatwedo/programmes/digitisation/content2011_2013/openlives.aspx

LLAS. Retrieved from https://www.llas.ac.uk

OpenLIVES project. Retrieved from https://www.llas.ac.uk/projects/OpenLIVES

Pretérito o Imperfecto. Humbox. Retrieved from http://humbox.ac.uk/3667/

Student interviews: studying history in action. Humbox. Retrieved from http://humbox.ac.uk/3654/

14 Discovering Spanish Voices Abroad in a Digital World

Antonio Martínez-Arboleda[1]

Abstract

This case study describes and assesses the Open Practice module *Discovering Spanish Voices Abroad in a Digital World*, one of the pedagogical applications of the JISC project OpenLIVES, which digitised Oral History interviews of Spanish migrants in the HumBox repository. This case study pays specific attention to learner production of Open Educational Resources. Through the process of production, learners developed their critical and practical understanding of Oral History and Migration by working with OpenLIVES interviews and other OER. Learners also carried out interviews with new research informants, produced their own audio documentaries on Spanish migration based on old and new interviews and finally published their outputs as OER. This case study demonstrates how the learners fulfill a virtuous circle of skills acquisition, meaningful learning and knowledge transfer, as they reuse OER and share their own research data, insights and knowledge with the open global community in OER repositories. Student generated materials were then added to the original collection of resources. The teacher offers a scaffolding of learning activities, team-work, support and feedback that enables the learners to make the most of this real life and ethical experience, whilst benefiting the wider community and giving the narratives of the migrants the credit they deserve.

Keywords: migration, oral history, documentaries, OER, interviews, research.

---

1. University of Leeds, UK; sllama@leeds.ac.uk

How to cite this chapter: Martínez-Arboleda, A. (2013). Discovering Spanish Voices Abroad in a Digital World. In A. Beaven, A. Comas-Quinn, & B. Sawhill (Eds), *Case Studies of Openness in the Language Classroom* (pp. 176-188). © Research-publishing.net.

1.   Context

Discovering Spanish Voices Abroad in a Digital World is a Spanish language in context module for Advanced learners. It started to be taught in October 2012 as a 4th Year option for all the University Degrees in Spanish at the University of Leeds. It is worth 20 credits (1/6 of a full-time year).

Figure 1.   OpenLIVES open learning resource in the HumBox
containing an interview[1]

This module was conceived as part of OpenLIVES project (Learning Insights from the Voices of Émigrés from Spain). One of the main outputs delivered by OpenLIVES is a collection of 19 digitised life story interviews featuring Spanish émigrés who left Spain between the end of the 1930's and the 1960's (Figure 1). Thanks to this project, the interviews, along with other ephemera, are available as OER in the HumBox repository. Such primary research data on migration can be used in the teaching of history, politics, economics, sociology, etc, and not only Languages and Area Studies. The other main set of outputs

---

1. Retrieved from http://humbox.ac.uk/3787/.

delivered by OpenLIVES is a series of suites of educational resources based on the re-use of the digitised life story interviews.

Figure 2. Collection of open learning resources
produced by teachers and students
in the Leeds module[1]

The module presented in this case study is the main OpenLIVES pedagogical application developed at the University of Leeds. There is a designated Collection of Resources (Figure 2) produced for this module both by the tutor and the students in the HumBox. This collection will grow with successive additions, as the module is intended to run on a permanent basis and will incorporate the research outputs of students of successive cohorts. A Year 1 Leeds OpenLIVES Collection in HumBox has been created for learners on other Spanish modules (Martínez-Arboleda, 2013d).

The OpenLIVES final year module fits in very well in the new University of Leeds Curriculum, which has been developed as part of the Curriculum Enhancement

---

1. University of Leeds (2013). Retrieved from http://humbox.ac.uk/4050/.

Project, in different ways: it promotes synoptic learning because it integrates skills and knowledge previously acquired across different subject areas; it incorporates a strong element of generic and subject-specific transferable skills, in an active and authentic way; and it promotes "research-based" teaching, which, according to the categorisation established by Healey and Jenkins (2009) in "Developing undergraduate research and enquiry", enables students to be the protagonists of their own research. In this respect, the contribution made by this course to Critical Pedagogy and the connections to the University of Lincoln Student as Producer Pedagogy have been explored by the author in the article "Liberation in OpenLIVES Critical Pedagogy: "empowerability" and critical action" (Martínez-Arboleda, 2013a).

2.   Intended outcomes

The teaching in the OpenLIVES module is underpinned by a detailed agenda in the fields of Open Practice, Socio-constructive Learning, Task-based Learning and Ethical Learning. Its main goal is to support students in their production of the following two outputs:

- A series of brand-new life story interviews with Spanish economic migrants who live in Leeds. These interviews are conducted in Spanish by the students (one interviewee per each three students). They are meant to be digitised and shared as OER by the students themselves in the HumBox and in Jorum, the national UK OER repository, at the end of the course, although they are carried out half way through the course. These outputs are not formally assessed.

- A 2,500 words (around 20 minutes) audio documentary in Spanish, one per student, to be submitted in its final version at the end of the course. The documentary incorporates soundtracks from the original OpenLIVES collection of interviews as well as from any new interviews conducted by the students themselves. The draft script of the documentary counts 40% towards the overall mark of the module and the second and final version, submitted in an audio file following feedback on the draft script, counts 30%.

Ultimately, this module is aimed at enabling students to become responsible digital scholars. At the end of the course, students should feel prepared to make tangible and socially purposeful contributions to the Global Community. In order to fulfil this greater goal and support student production, the module intends to provide students with skills in the following areas:

- oral history interviewing and coding (research methods);

- documentary scripting and production, including using the software Audacity;

- OER literacy, including publishing and licensing;

- team work and project management;

- Spanish language for specific purposes.

The module also promotes critical and ethical understanding of all the social, epistemological and educational issues connected to the research and production work carried out by students. This means that the teaching programme also touches upon the following areas:

- OER and open practice from a social, educational and political point of view;

- economic migration in Spain in the 21st century, mainly in comparison with 1960's economic migration;

- the economic, political and social situation in contemporary Spain;

- ethical protocols for research;

- oral history, from a social, scientific and ethical point of view;

- modes of expression and the documentary genre.

Half way through the course, before the interviews, students write a 750-word research report explaining and justifying, academically, their next steps in the research project, namely the interviews and the documentaries. After the interviews have been carried out, students report again, this time 10 minutes orally, on their research progress. These two pieces of work are assessed and count 15% of the overall mark for the module each.

Figure 3.   OpenLIVES cycle in the Leeds module[1]

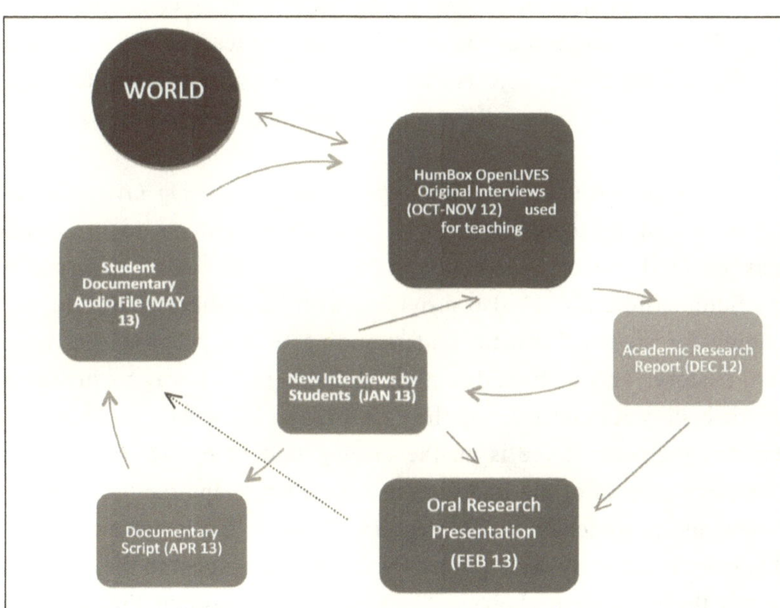

The diagram in Figure 3 above shows the flows and feeds of the research production and knowledge transfer cycle that takes place in the module. Its

1. Retrieved from http://revistacaracteres.net/revista/vol2n1mayo2013/liberation-in-openlives-critical-pedagogy-empowerability-and-critical-action/.

final outcomes (the interviews, the teaching materials and the documentaries) incorporate the research and reflections of the students and the teacher, including the feedback. The ultimate goal is to incorporate the new interviews and the documentaries produced by students into the HumBox OpenLIVES collections and Jorum. Feedback is always provided before students move on to the next steps.

3.   Nuts and bolts

The module requires a great degree of readiness to broaden one's professional scope and involve other colleagues in its preparation and delivery. At first sight this is simply a Language in Context module with a strong component of Open Practice. However, as soon as the work unfolds, the teacher will feel the need and desire to learn about subjects that traditionally are not related to language teaching such as Oral History, Research Methods and Research Ethics.

Life history research in educational settings: learning from Lives (Goodson, 2001) is one of the core readings. It introduces students to the practical aspects of Oral History Methodology in an intellectually inspiring way. Penny Summerfield (2011) also provides, with her insightful lecture, a firm grounding for students' critical understanding of the purpose and methods of Oral History: This distinct discipline is an alternative way to "traditional" academic history for constructing the past through life stories. In Oral History interviews, the interviewee is on the driving seat of his/her own narrative. The research agenda of the interviewer should not shape the outcome of the interview and is somehow tacitly negotiated during the interview. Crucially, Oral History is ethically underpinned by the utmost respect to the individuals' lives and their narrative choices. Therefore it is important that students in this module understand the differences between qualitative research methods interviews and life story (Oral History) interviews as well as the points in common. In the Collection of Resources produced for this module, readers can find the materials that have been used for the teaching of Qualitative Research Methods and Oral History.

Equally, the boundaries between journalist interviews and life story (Oral History) interviews must be set very clearly when producing the documentaries, in which extracts from life story interviews are to be used. That is why during the second part of the module, once the interviews have been carried out and processed, students learn about aural genres, journalistic reporting and academically produced history for wider audiences.

When it comes to supporting students ahead of their writing-up of the script for the documentary, there is a great emphasis on their freedom to choose their target audience and the ways in which they would engage with it. Students are encouraged to reflect upon different formats and are allowed to challenge established documentary genres if they wish so, always in a purposeful way. At the same time, since the documentary incorporates extracts from life story interviews, students have to respect the spirit of the narration of the interviewees when building their own narrative in the script. All the interviewees' statements used for the documentary have to maintain the original meaning and sense when incorporated into it. There is a useful list of resources and readings on documentaries, genres and history dissemination in the HumBox (Martínez-Arboleda, 2013b).

Finally, the OER publication and licensing is taught in a very traditional way: the different licenses and their purpose are explained; students' practical understanding of their meaning and functions is tested; the concept of OER "quality" in relation to different uses and users is discussed, following the work of Kelty, Burrus and Baraniuk (2008); and a critical overview of the available repositories for dissemination of their interviews and documentaries is also offered.

4.   In practice

Before the teaching started, the module leader had to seek ethical approval for the Oral History research that would be carried out by the students. This involved filling in a form in which the purpose of the project and the methodology are explained to the Research Ethics Committee of the Faculty. In the form, the module leader must also provide details of how research participants are going to be recruited, what written information is going to be given to the potential participants who respond to the advert, what consent forms the participants will be signing and how all the data obtained is going to be stored or disseminated. This type of ethical review procedure is very common in research projects, less so as part of teaching.

This application for ethical approval process is an essential part of the work of any researcher when working with human subjects in a real life experience. For anyone intending for the first time in their careers to offer their students the opportunity of carrying out this type of research, filling the form is a very formative and almost essential experience. In fact, the application form for ethical approval itself and the relevant correspondence with the Research Ethics Committee, which includes the letter granting approval, have been used as learning materials for the students. Nothing can beat authenticity and transparency, particularly if the idea is that students carry out their research with a good deal of autonomy. By sharing and discussing all this information with students, they acquire ownership of the research project. From that point in the course, any other documentation for the project has to be produced by the team. In the case of this module, students discussed and drafted the consent forms in two languages and created and distributed the advert for potential participants. The text of the email to be sent to individuals showing an interest to participate in the research was also drafted by the students. In all cases, the tutor reviewed and edited as appropriate. The consent forms and other related documents have been published as an OER in the Collection of Resources of the module in HumBox.

In order to scaffold all the learning in the module, the sessions had to be varied in their format and delivery throughout the course: from lectures to project management meetings, language learning workshops and seminars. Each one of the sessions is almost unique in its approach and methodology because the content and the skills are diverse and the main student-produced output is relatively complex.

During January 2013 two life story (Oral History) interviews were conducted, recorded and transcribed by the students. The interviewees, two young people from Spain who now live in Leeds were interviewed separately. The contents of the interviews are hugely interesting and revealing, both as personal stories and as true snapshots of the life, problems and expectations of economic migrants, often misconstrued by the media. They can be used for the study of a wide range of topics and certainly for advanced language work. Both participants agreed to publish, as OER, the full audio file and the transcripts under their real names. Student produced interviews and documentaries can be found in the Collection of Resources.

The publication of these interviews by the students, as well as the ensuing documentaries, only takes place between the end of the course, in May, and the graduation of the student, in July. The reason is that it is felt at this stage that the students who conducted and transcribed the interviews and produced the documentaries should only give their consent and share the resources once the course is finished and the results have been published and before they officially cease to be students. There are powerful ethical and educational reasons behind this decision. There should not be pressure on students for them to publish something that they later may regret having shared, particularly if they may have done it to please their OER-enthusiast tutor.

5.   Conclusion

One of the interesting features of this module is that it can be downsized or reshaped by combining the different components at ease. Also, this course has been delivered almost exclusively with OER and other free access online resources. The Research Methods materials of Learning from WoerK (University of Plymouth) hosted in Jorum proved very useful. There are also key materials from the Universities of Manchester, Leicester and Huddersfield and from different academics and organisations in Spain, UK and Argentina that can be found online, as it can be seen in the Collection of Resources.

Student Open Practice in this course has played a crucial role. Many key decisions in the course are taken by the students in conjunction with the tutor. Students shared their interim research reports and worked in teams in a wide range of tasks. In this context of collaboration, a student from Communication Studies at the University of Leeds decided to help the students in the OpenLIVES module. He shared with them, internally, his assessed coursework: a radio documentary on recent Spanish economic migration in the UK.

The most distinctive feature of OpenLIVES in relation to other OER and OP is that it has penetrated in several areas that are outside the traditional scope of OER and OP studies, hence introducing OER and OP to "non-OER" tutors and academics. OpenLIVES has contributed to current debates about the role of students in Higher Education and research-based teaching and on the integration of language and cultural content. OpenLIVES has also initiated other debates on issues such as the purpose of student coursework, student production of OER, redefinition and integration of "employable" skills ("empowerability") or the role of Oral History in Higher Education.

There has been a great interest in this module as well as on the other OpenLIVES pedagogical applications at Southampton and Portsmouth. The number of scholarly presentations and articles on the OpenLIVES Pedagogy continues to grow (Martínez-Arboleda, 2013c). Successive cohorts of students at Leeds, and hopefully beyond, will be incorporating more and more resources to this collection. The author has received enquiries from teachers and researchers who want to explore further this open methodology as well as very promising feedback from existing and potential informants and students.

Acknowledgements. The author would like to thank the University of Southampton team, made up of Pedro García Guirao, Irina Nelson, Kate Borthwick and Ali Dickens, and Miguel Arrebola, from the University of Portsmouth, for their enthusiastic and illuminating contributions to this module. The generous contribution of Dr Alicia Pozo-Gutiérrez is worth noting. Alicia's reading lists and handouts for her Final Year course on Migration at the University of Southampton were of great help when designing the University of Leeds module.

The involvement of Dr Javier López Alos, visiting fellow at the University of Leeds, in the delivery of one session on Spanish Migration in the 1960's and his selection of key audiovisual materials enriched greatly the course too.

References

Goodson, I. F. (2001). *Life history research in educational settings: learning from Lives*. Buckingham: Open University Press.

Healey, M., & Jenkins, A. (2009). Developing undergraduate research and enquiry. *The Higher Education Academy*. Retrieved from http://www.heacademy.ac.uk/assets/documents/research/DevelopingUndergraduateResearchandInquiry.pdf

Kelty, C., Burrus, S., & Baraniuk, R. (2008). Peer Review Anew: Three Principles and a Case Study in Postpublication Quality Assurance. *Proceedings of the IEEE, 96*(6). Retrieved from http://cnx.org/news/news/peer-review-anew-ProcIEEE-june08.pdf

Martínez-Arboleda, A. (2013a). Liberation in OpenLIVES Critical Pedagogy: "empowerability" and critical action. *Caracteres. Estudios culturales y críticos de la esfera digital, 2* (1). Retrieved from http://revistacaracteres.net/revista/vol2n1mayo2013/liberation-in-openlives-critical-pedagogy-empowerability-and-critical-action/

Martínez-Arboleda, A. (2013b). Resources for the session on documentaries in the OpenLIVES module "Discovering Spanish Voices Abroad in a Digital World", University of Leeds (SPPO3640). Retrieved from http://humbox.ac.uk/4063/

Martínez-Arboleda, A. (2013c). Leeds OpenLIVES Academic Presentations. Retrieved from http://humbox.ac.uk/4062/

Martínez-Arboleda, A. (2013d). *OpenLIVES - Year 1 Spanish Language and Spanish Society Learning Resources*. Retrieved from http://humbox.ac.uk/4051/

Summerfield, P. (2011). What is Oral History? *methods@manchester: research methods in social sciences*. Retrieved from http://www.methods.manchester.ac.uk/methods/oralhistory/

Other resources

OpenLIVES project. (2012). An open collection of research data and teaching materials relating to Spanish migrant stories. JISC. *OpenLIVES Spanish emigre interviews – JISC 2012*. Retrieved from http://humbox.ac.uk/3790/

OpenLIVES project. (2012). OpenLIVES Spanish emigre interviews - Germinal Luis Fernandez. [screenshot]. An open collection of research data and teaching materials relating to Spanish migrant stories. JISC. Retrieved from http://humbox.ac.uk/3787/

University of Leeds. (2013). *Consent Forms, Advert and Letter of Information for Oral History Research Interview, Publication of Life Story as OER and Publication of Life Story Documentary as OER*. Retrieved from http://humbox.ac.uk/4058/

University of Leeds. (2013). OpenLIVES - Discovering Spanish Voices Abroad in a Digital World: Resources. Retrieved from http://humbox.ac.uk/4050/

Useful links

Audacity: http://audacity.sourceforge.net/

JISC. (2011). The OpenLIVES Project. Retrieved from http://www.jisc.ac.uk/whatwedo/programmes/digitisation/content2011_2013/openlives.aspx

Jorum: http://jorum.ac.uk/

LLAS. Centre for Languages, Linguistics and Area Studies. (2012). The OpenLIVES Project. Retrieved from https://www.llas.ac.uk/projects/OpenLIVES

The HumBox: http://humbox.ac.uk/

University of Leeds. (2013). Curriculum Enhancement Project. Retrieved from http://curriculum.leeds.ac.uk/

University of Lincoln. (2013). *Student as Producer*. Retrieved from http://studentasproducer.lincoln.ac.uk/

Collaborative Italian:
An Open Online Language Course

Cecilia Goria[1]

Abstract

The focus of this case study is on the design and content of a module in Italian language, *Collaborative Italian* (*Collit*), which provides the empirical ground to implement open and student-led learning. *Collit* is an online learning initiative which targets adult students with at least an Intermediate (B1) level of Italian. It is free, optional and non-credit bearing. Most significantly, *Collit* is open in content and practice. By exploiting the openness and the flexibility of the online environment, *Collit* provides the learners with an overall communicative language learning experience based on collaboration and social interaction. *Collit*'s central activities pivot around a wiki task for which the learners take responsibility for their learning outcomes by developing their own learning content in accordance with their needs and interests. That is, the learners actively contribute to *Collit*'s curriculum by using open online resources to create new learning materials to be shared within the learning community. The result is increased engagement, participation and involvement with the learning process for the benefit of language achievement. The aim of this contribution is to present *Collit* by focussing on its design, its content and practice and to reflect on the affordances and limitations that have emerged from it.

Keywords: openness, collaboration, learner-generated content, online learning, MOOC, language learning.

---

1. University of Nottingham, Nottingham, UK; cecilia.goria@nottingham.ac.uk

How to cite this chapter: Goria, C. (2013). Collaborative Italian: An Open Online Language Course. In A. Beaven, A. Comas-Quinn, & B. Sawhill (Eds), *Case Studies of Openness in the Language Classroom* (pp. 189-201). © Research-publishing.net.

---

1.   Context

The purpose of this contribution is to present a case study in which pedagogical practices based on the use of Web 2.0 applications, such as wikis, are applied in the context of language learning. The attention is on the design and content of an open online module in Italian language, called *Collaborative Italian* (*Collit*), which provides the empirical context for adopting a student-led learning approach while experimenting with openness.

The notion of openness has received increasing attention in education with the development of Open Courses, Open Educational Resources and Open Access. The recent rise and spread of MOOCs (Massive Open Online Courses) and the pedagogical model that they promote (Cormier & Siemens, 2010) are amongst the latest expressions of such a trend.

MOOCs recruit globally, are taught online and require no institutional affiliation. They are available to any individuals wishing to register regardless of their professional or academic experience. MOOCs promote participatory and connectivist pedagogies which exploit the openness and the multimediality of the online environment for building connections and for constructing and sharing knowledge.

Although *Collit* is not a fully-fledged MOOC, mainly because of its small size – a few regular participants against the hundreds in MOOCs (the term T(iny)OOCs (Goria, 2012) may be more appropriate), it incorporates several features of MOOC pedagogy. In particular, like a MOOC, *Collit* is open in content and practice.

Collit is an online language module run by the Language Centre (LC), School of Cultures, Languages and Area Studies at the University of Nottingham (UoN). The LC offers three levels of face-to-face inter faculty modules in Italian: Beginners (A1); Elementary (A2) and Intermediate (B1). Additionally, with *Collit*, the LC currently teaches learners with levels of Italian above Intermediate (B1).

Collit's rationale lies in the need to expand the LC Italian provision and cater for more advanced learners. Every academic year there is a small group of learners, especially exchange students, who come to UoN and wish to take Italian as part of their study programme. Their linguistic proficiency varies greatly depending on whether they have studied Italian at university or in secondary school, or whether they have learnt the language in informal contexts, for instance by living in Italy or by coming from families in which one of the parents is Italian. Different learning backgrounds lead to the development of different skills. Generally, those who learn Italian in informal contexts are more proficient in speaking and listening than those who take formal lessons and who perform better in writing and grammatical accuracy.

As the LC offered only the three stages listed above, these advanced learners were unable to pursue their interest in the Italian language, because their number was insufficient to financially justify fully-fledged face-to-face modules. Thus, the LC regularly faced the dilemma of whether to turn these learners away or attempt to accommodate them within the existing provision. *Collit* was conceived to address these problems: to cater for these advanced learners, to cope with mixed abilities and to affect minimally the institutional resources.

Collit complies with the following institutional criteria:

- it is a 12 week module to fit the university schedule;

- it is an inter faculty module offered to learners from a diverse range of study programmes at all levels of their studies;

- it is offered as an elective module.

In addition, *Collit* is non-credit bearing, allowing autonomy from institutional requirements such as high-stakes assessment, a pre-defined curriculum to fit in with other modules, minimum number of teaching hours, and so forth[1].

---

1. It should be noted that after two semesters (Autumn and Spring Semesters 2011-2012) as non-credit bearing, *Collit* became a credit-bearing module in the academic year 2012-2013. This changed its nature significantly. A discussion of the impact of such a change is beyond the scope of this contribution.

It is taught entirely online to avoid difficulties with classroom and timetable availability, and is offered openly to off campus participants not registered at UoN. *Collit* does not include formal assessment. Instead, all *Collit* activities incorporate strategies of learning oriented and less hierarchical forms of assessment (Carless, 2007).

Finally, the relatively high language level required by *Collit* imposes restrictions on the number of eligible participants, who are recruited on the basis of an interview with the teacher who evaluates the level of comprehension and fluency in the target language. So far, *Collit*'s regular participants have been one ex-student, three registered students of UoN, one retired and one in-service member of staff.

2. Intended outcomes: *Collit*'s learning outcomes and pedagogical objectives

The context described above led to the design of a flexible module which runs online, recruits openly, is optional and non-credit bearing. It is also open-curricular and develops entirely from the learners' participation and contributions. *Collit* has several student-controlled learning outcomes (LOs):

1. further development of language skills (listening, reading, speaking and writing);

2. improved ability to deal adequately with real-life situations in the target language;

3. improved awareness of several aspects of the Italian culture and society;

4. consolidated and extended knowledge of the grammar of Italian.

The overarching objective of *Collit* is to ensure learners' achievement of the LOs listed above through an informal communicative experience. This is done by adopting an approach to course design which promotes collaboration, knowledge sharing, social interaction, learning which is personally relevant, self and peer assessment, and learner-teacher mutual respect and openness (Toohey, 1999). Thus, advocating the role of the teacher as the source of guidance for learners' own initiative, *Collit*'s intended pedagogical objectives (IPOs) are:

1. to enhance communication through social interaction and collaboration;

2. to encourage self and peer assessment;

3. to improve ownership of learning;

4. to increase knowledge which is personally relevant.

These are achieved by exploiting the openness and flexibility of the online environment mainly through wiki activities and synchronous voiced communication.

The wiki provides the learners with the environment to improve their language skills and awareness (LOs above) through individual practice as well as sharing and collaboration (IPO 1).

For the wiki task the learners are required to search for, evaluate, select and share online resources to develop themes in accordance with their own needs and interests. Beyond providing the participants with a broadly defined initial structure of suggested themes, the wiki is open-ended and develops entirely from student-led learning activities. In this sense *Collit* implements the *community-as-curriculum* model (Cormier & Siemens, 2010, p. 35) of open courses such as MOOCs, by which the position of the curriculum is inverted from being a prerequisite to being the output of the module. As in a MOOC, in *Collit*, under the educator's guidance, "learners are expected to actively contribute to the formation of the curriculum through conversations, discussions and interactions" (ibid, p. 36) through sharing resources and creating new ones. In such a context the learners determine their own learning trajectories (IPOs 3 and 4 above) on the basis of their existing skills and those to be improved. This addresses the issue of mixed abilities mentioned earlier.

The open-ended nature of *Collit* is maximised by engaging the participants not only in discerning content and resources, but also in taking up the role of teachers and creating new materials and activities for their peers' learning. The process of creating rather than responding to questions leads to deep learning (Draper, 2009) and increases the participants' ownership of the learning process (IPOs 3 and 4).

As the wiki allows all users to have equal and open authoring access, it ensures that all learning content is available for follow-up activities of self and peer assessment (IPO 2).

Sharing and collaboration in *Collit* is also supported by synchronous voiced *Skype* tutorials held in a group. The aim of these meetings is to provide speaking practice (LOs above), increase social presence, provide timely teacher support and stimulate learners' initiative[1].

3.   Nuts and bolts

Collit develops around a website, *Skype* tutorials and a wiki. *Collit*'s website is used by the teacher to deliver information and instructions about the module. A free website creator (www.weebly.com) is used, one which allows the creation of websites which are simple to design, build and maintain.

The *Skype* tutorials run once a week using *Skype Premium* because it supports group video chats. *Skype* voice only is also used when connection problems arise. Other video conferencing platforms have been tested, but *Skype* has turned out to be the most effective and easy to use.

---

1. The participants also keep a reflective journal of their experience providing opportunities for self-evaluation. The learners choose the format of their journal. As the journal has not played a key role in *Collit* so far, it will not be discussed in this contribution.

Pbworks (www.pbworks.com) is *Collit*'s wiki platform. The learners have full editor access in order to be able to populate it with their chosen learning resources and those newly created. Pbworks was selected because of its accessible design and editing tools.

4.   In practice

This section presents some activities of *Collit* as the practical implementation of the *community-as-curriculum* model and as practical examples of learner-generated teaching content, i.e. exercises for language practice.

4.1.   Community-as-curriculum

As mentioned earlier, the learners populate the wiki with content of their choice after negotiation with the teacher. The topics are explored and discussed during the *Skype* sessions and subsequently the learners look for relevant resources and create new related activities.

In one instance, during a *Skype* tutorial, the conversation verged towards the topic of social networks and one learner was particularly interested in the development of *Facebook* and the biography of Mark Zuckerberg. It was agreed that he would explore this topic as part of an individual work task – to be carried out during the first three weeks of the module[1]. First, the learner produced and published an essay on the chosen topic. The teacher gave feedback on his work which was again openly discussed in a *Skype* session. Second, as the learner mentioned a number of additional resources on the topic, he was encouraged to explore them further. The learner found a 50 minute interview on *YouTube* about Mark Zuckerberg and used it to produce further written work. It is worth pointing out that this particular learner's level of spoken Italian was very high, while he needed to work on his writing skills.

---

1. It is important to clarify that, although the students begin participating in *Collit* with individual tasks, all resources are shared and all students are encouraged to view and comment on each other's work.

A similar approach is used for the study of grammar. All learners negotiate with the teacher the grammar topics of their choice and look for and create new grammar resources. One learner created and shared a new wiki page with the explanation of the grammatical rules of the use of the past conditional (Figure 1).

Figure 1.   A learner's explanations on a wiki page

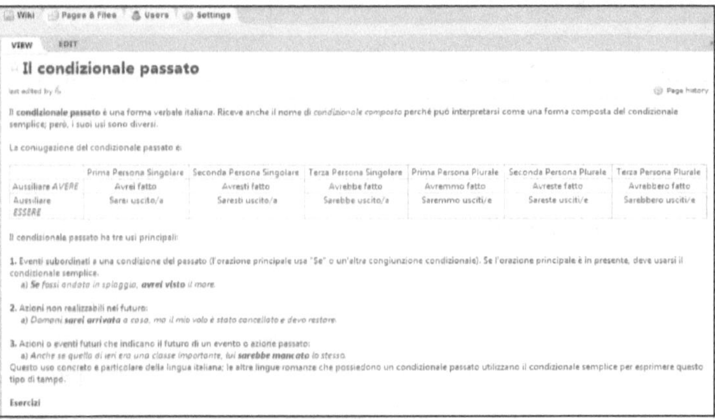

Wiki | Pages & Files | Users | Settings

VIEW | EDIT

Il condizionale passato

last edited by &

Page history

Il **condizionale passato** è una forma verbale italiana. Riceve anche il nome di *condizionale composto* perché può interpretarsi come una forma composta del condizionale semplice; però, i suoi usi sono diversi.

La coniugazione del condizionale passato è:

	Prima Persona Singolare	Seconda Persona Singolare	Terza Persona Singolare	Prima Persona Plurale	Seconda Persona Plurale	Terza Persona Plurale
Aussiliare *AVERE*	Avrei fatto	Avresti fatto	Avrebbe fatto	Avremmo fatto	Avreste fatto	Avrebbero fatto
Aussiliare *ESSERE*	Sarei uscito/a	Saresti uscito/a	Sarebbe uscito/a	Saremmo usciti/e	Sareste usciti/e	Sarebbero usciti/e

Il condizionale passato ha tre usi principali:

1. Eventi subordinati a una condizione del passato (l'orazione principale usa "Se" o un'altra congiunzione condizionale). Se l'orazione principale è in presente, deve usarsi il condizionale semplice.
    a) *Se fossi andato in spiaggia*, **avrei visto** *il mare.*

2. Azioni non realizzabili nel futuro:
    a) *Domani* **sarei arrivata** *a casa, ma il mio volo è stato cancellato e devo restare.*

3. Azioni o eventi futuri che indicano il futuro di un evento o azione passato:
    a) *Anche se quello di ieri era una classe importante, lui* **sarebbe mancato** *lo stesso.*
Questo uso concreto e particolare della lingua italiana; le altre lingue romanze che possiedono un condizionale passato utilizzano il condizionale semplice per esprimere questo tipo di tempo.

Esercizi

In addition, the same learner decided to carry out a small comparative study between the use of the same verb form in Italian and in her native language (Figure 2), and finally shared it with the others.

Figure 2.   A learner's contribution

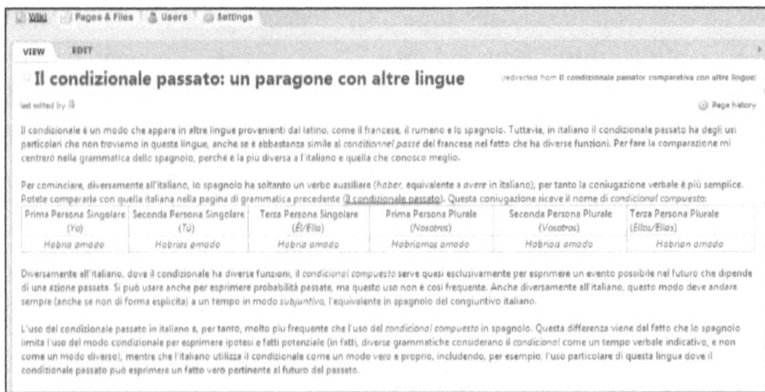

Wiki | Pages & Files | Users | Settings

VIEW | EDIT

Il condizionale passato: un paragone con altre lingue

(redirected from Il condizionale passato: comparativa con altre lingue)

last edited by &

Page history

Il condizionale è un modo che appare in altre lingue provenienti dal latino, come il francese, il rumeno e lo spagnolo. Tuttavia, in italiano il condizionale passato ha degli usi particolari che non troviamo in questa lingue, anche se è abbastanza simile al *conditionnel passé* del francese nel fatto che ha diverse funzioni. Per fare la comparazione mi centrerò nella grammatica dello spagnolo, perché e la più diversa a l'italiano e quella che conosco meglio.

Per cominciare, diversamente all'italiano, lo spagnolo ha soltanto un verbo aussiliare (*haber*, equivalente a *avere* in italiano), per tanto la coniugazione verbale è più semplice. Potete compararla con quella italiana nella pagina di grammatica precedente (Il condizionale passato). Questa coniugazione riceve il nome di *condicional compuesto*:

Prima Persona Singolare (Yo)	Seconda Persona Singolare (Tú)	Terza Persona Singolare (Él/Ella)	Prima Persona Plurale (Nosotros)	Seconda Persona Plurale (Vosotros)	Terza Persona Plurale (Ellos/Ellas)
Habria amado	*Habrias amado*	*Habria amado*	*Habriamos amado*	*Habriais amado*	*Habrian amado*

Diversamente all'italiano, dove il condizionale ha diverse funzioni, il *condicional compuesto* serve quasi esclusivamente per esprimere un evento possibile nel futuro che dipende di una azione passata. Si può usare anche per esprimere probabilità passate, ma questo uso non è così frequente. Anche diversamente all'italiano, questo modo deve andare sempre (anche se non di forma esplicita) a un tempo in modo *subjuntivo*, l'equivalente in spagnolo del congiuntivo italiano.

L'uso del condizionale passato in italiano è, per tanto, molto più frequente che l'uso del *condicional compuesto* in spagnolo. Questa differenza viene dal fatto che lo spagnolo limita l'uso del modo condizionale per esprimere ipotesi e fatti potenziale (in fatti, diverse grammatiche considerano il *condicional* come un tempo verbale indicativo, e non come un modo diverso), mentre che l'italiano utilizza il condizionale come un modo vero e proprio, includendo, per esempio, l'uso particolare di questa lingua dove il condizionale passato può esprimere un fatto vero pertinente al futuro del passato.

4.2.   Learner-generated teaching resources

The next example illustrates a set of learning events in which the learners engaged in searching for content and in creating new activities, which were later used by the other participants as study materials.

After a visit to Italy, one learner chose to share one aspect of his experience with the other participants. He did so by selecting a relevant *YouTube* video and by creating a set of related comprehension questions. Additional questions were also posted by the teacher (circled). Both media and set of questions were published on the wiki for the other learners to view and complete the task respectively (Figure 3).

Figure 3.   Study materials produced by a learner

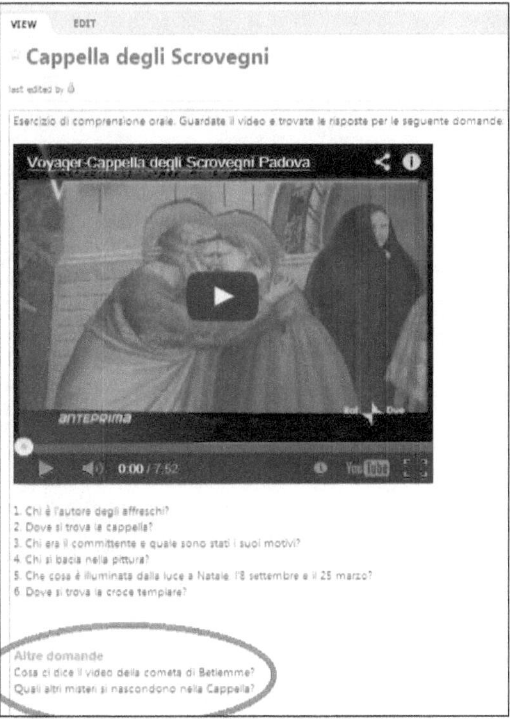

The responses of the participants were different in nature. Some language corrections were suggested, the comprehension questions were answered and new related resources and learner-created activities were added: one learner added a new related *YouTube* video and a new set of comprehension questions; another learner added a *PowerPoint* presentation on the work of an Italian painter and a related piece of written work, generating additional participation and learning resources. In this instance, the teacher also took the role of the learner by completing all comprehension tasks, providing model answers for self-assessment. Finally, all learners worked collaboratively to create a glossary of the vocabulary related to the topic Art.

Similarly, with reference to grammar, one learner chose to work on the use of the Italian past tenses. She looked for an appropriate text and created a Fill in the Gap exercise (Figure 4). This time the teacher intervened with model answers after all learners had attempted the exercise and had given feedback on each other's answers.

Figure 4.   Gap-fill created by a learner

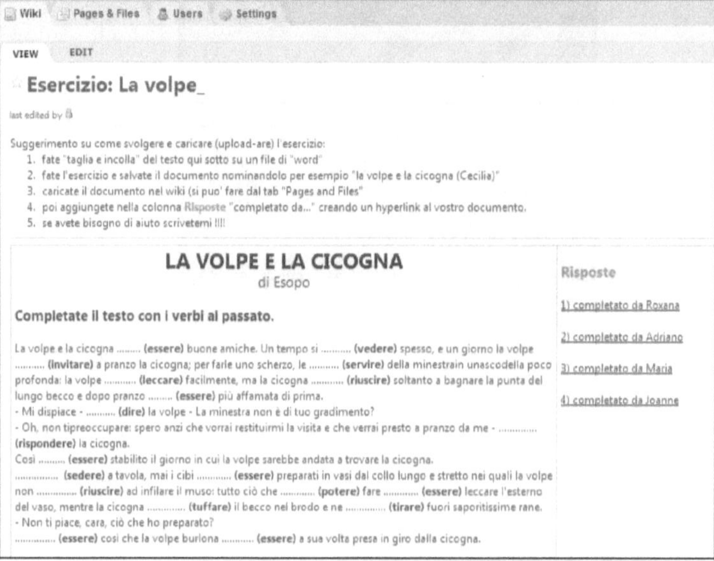

Wiki   Pages & Files   Users   Settings

VIEW   EDIT

Esercizio: La volpe_

last edited by

Suggerimento su come svolgere e caricare (upload-are) l'esercizio:
1. fate "taglia e incolla" del testo qui sotto su un file di "word"
2. fate l'esercizio e salvate il documento nominandolo per esempio "la volpe e la cicogna (Cecilia)"
3. caricate il documento nel wiki (si puo' fare dal tab "Pages and Files"
4. poi aggiungete nella colonna Risposte "completato da..." creando un hyperlink al vostro documento.
5. se avete bisogno di aiuto scrivetemi !!!!

LA VOLPE E LA CICOGNA
di Esopo

Completate il testo con i verbi al passato.

La volpe e la cicogna .... (**essere**) buone amiche. Un tempo si .... (**vedere**) spesso, e un giorno la volpe .... (**invitare**) a pranzo la cicogna; per farle uno scherzo, le .... (**servire**) della minestrain unascodella poco profonda: la volpe .... (**leccare**) facilmente, ma la cicogna .... (**riuscire**) soltanto a bagnare la punta del lungo becco e dopo pranzo .... (**essere**) più affamata di prima.
- Mi dispiace - .... (**dire**) la volpe - La minestra non è di tuo gradimento?
- Oh, non tipreoccupare: spero anzi che vorrai restituirmi la visita e che verrai presto a pranzo da me - .... (**rispondere**) la cicogna.
Così .... (**essere**) stabilito il giorno in cui la volpe sarebbe andata a trovare la cicogna.
.... (**sedere**) a tavola, mai i cibi .... (**essere**) preparati in vasi dal collo lungo e stretto nei quali la volpe non .... (**riuscire**) ad infilare il muso: tutto ciò che .... (**potere**) fare .... (**essere**) leccare l'esterno del vaso, mentre la cicogna .... (**tuffare**) il becco nel brodo e ne .... (**tirare**) fuori saporitissime rane.
- Non ti piace, cara, ciò che ho preparato?
.... (**essere**) così che la volpe burlona .... (**essere**) a sua volta presa in giro dalla cicogna.

Risposte

1) completato da Roxana

2) completato da Adriano

3) completato da Maria

4) completato da Joanne

5. Conclusion: Open *Collit*

It was mentioned earlier that in addition to the learning outcomes, *Collit* has several pedagogical objectives (cf. IPOs in section 2). These are achieved by adopting features of the open pedagogical model promoted by MOOCs (Cormier & Siemens, 2010). Like a MOOC, *Collit* embraces openness in a number of ways. *Collit*:

- is taught online and recruits openly, provided the learners have the appropriate level of linguistic competence, aiming to ensure variety and continuity in the social interaction;

- relies on freely accessible online applications keeping the impact of the running of the module to the minimum;

- relies on existing open online resources and generates new ones, ensuring the benefits of multimodal and multimedia learning (Moreno & Mayer, 1999);

- is based on open and transparent dialogues between the learners and between the learners and the teacher, encouraging knowledge sharing, collaboration and reflection on one's own work and that of others;

- implements the *community-as-curriculum* model of MOOCs.

The examples in section 4 show that open practices have so far proved successful for nurturing new learning dynamics by which the learners create their own learning content and lead their learning process.

However, other factors related to openness have had a less positive impact. It is attested that learners' persistence and motivation is lower in online than in face-to-face programmes (Park & Choi, 2009; Rovai, 2002; among others). The online nature of *Collit* coupled with its optionality has caused slow student responses, intermittent participation and several dropouts. Also, *Collit's* open recruitment strategy has increased the degree of mixed abilities amongst the learners. This, added to the fact that the learners have different backgrounds and ages, made it difficult to reconcile their abilities and interests, affecting the creation of the materials. Similarly, the varying levels of digital skills of the learners made it difficult to overcome technical glitches and influenced the teacher's choice of e-tools. Although the participants were expected to feel comfortable with the use of online tools, technology was kept as simple as possible to help reduce technical problems, limiting the variety of *Collit*'s learning activities.

These observations will provide guidelines for the future phases of *Collit* and for future studies concerned with the adoption of open pedagogies for language learning and teaching.

References

Carless, D. (2007). Learning-oriented assessment: conceptual bases and practical implications. *Innovations in Education and Teaching International, 44*(1), 57-66.

Cormier, D., & Siemens, G. (2010). The Open course through the open door: open course as research, learning and engagement. *Educause Review*, 31-39. Retrieved from http://net. educause.edu/ir/library/pdf/ERM1042.pdf

Draper, S. W. (2009). Catalytic assessment: understanding how MCQs can foster deep learning. *British Journal of Education Technology (special issue on e-assessment), 40*(2), 285-293.

Goria, C. (2012). *Collaborative Italian - Pedagogy 2.0 for student-led language teaching.* Paper presented at Learning Through Sharing: Open Resources, Open Practices, Open Communication. Eurocall CMC & Teacher Education SIGs Annual Workshop, Bologna/ Italy, 29-30 March 2012.

Moreno, R., & Mayer, R. E. (1999). Cognitive Principles of Multimedia Learning. The Role of Modality and Contiguity. *Journal of Educational Psychology, 91*(2), 358-368.

Park, J.-H., & Choi, H. J. (2009). Factors influencing adult learners' decision to drop out or persist in online learning. *Educational Technology & Society, 12*(4), 207-217.

Rovai, A. P. (2002). Sense of community, perceived cognitive learning, and persistence in asynchronous learning netwworks. *Internet and Higher Edication, 5*, 319-332.

Toohey, S. (1999). Beliefs, values and ideologies in course design. In S. Toohey (Ed.), *Designing courses for higher education* (44-69). Buckingham: The Society for Research into Higher Education and Open University Press.

Section 5.

Learner Autonomy

16 When Learner Autonomy Meets Open Educational Resources: A Study of a Self-learning Environment for Italian as a Foreign Language

Marco Cappellini[1]

Abstract

The aim of this case study is twofold. On the one hand, it shows a possible use of Open Educational Resources in a self-learning environment as it has been done at Lille 3 University since 2006 (Rivens Mompean & Eisenbeis, 2009). On the other hand, it highlights some of the relations between OER appropriation and the development of learner autonomy. Learner autonomy is defined as the capacity of a learner to take responsibility and control of his/her own learning process. This includes establishing learning goals, developing learning strategies, finding relevant OER, and self-assessing the effectiveness of the learning process (Holec, 1981). During the past years, many researchers and practitioners have argued that OER could play a crucial role in learner autonomy development (Barbot & Camatarri, 1999). This paper considers some necessary conditions for this to happen, the most important of which is the teacher's and the peers' mediation necessary for learners to make the most of OER.

Keywords: learner autonomy, self-learning, OER, open educational resources, affordance, mediation.

1. Joint Research Unit Savoirs Textes Langage (STL), UMR 8163 National Scientific Council (CNRS), Lille 3 University, Lille, France; marco.cappellini@univ-lille3.fr

How to cite this chapter: Cappellini, M. (2013). When Learner Autonomy Meets Open Educational Resources: A Study of a Self-learning Environment for Italian as a Foreign Language. In A. Beaven, A. Comas-Quinn, & B. Sawhill (Eds), *Case Studies of Openness in the Language Classroom* (pp. 205-216). © Research-publishing.net.

1.   Context

This case study presents the possible relations built between Open Educational Resources (OER) and the development of learner autonomy in a self-learning course at Lille 3 University. We suggest that OER can be a tool to develop learner autonomy, but only under certain conditions, including a variety of OER types and the mediation of a teacher or a tutor.

In the first section, we present the post-graduate curriculum in foreign language pedagogy at Lille 3 University and the role the self-learning course has in it. In the second section, we define learner autonomy as opposed to heteronomy and anomy. In the third section, we show the structure of the self-learning course and how OER are used according to the learner autonomy paradigm. In the fourth section, we analyze an example where the development of a student's learner autonomy is intertwined with instrumental genesis of OER based on their learning affordances.

At Lille 3 University, students in foreign language pedagogy at a post-graduate level have, among other courses, a course of self-learning in a foreign language. In this self-learning course, each student chooses a foreign language he/she wants to learn and learns it autonomously with the counselling of a teacher/ tutor. Different foreign languages have been proposed during the years: English, French, Spanish, Italian and Polish. Even if the number of OER available for these languages is very different, the self-learning course has the same structure for every learner and students go through the same learning stages (see Section 3).

The main objective of the post-graduate curriculum in foreign language pedagogy at Lille 3 University is for the students to become pedagogical engineers, able to design, build and run self-learning environments integrating Information and Communication Technologies and to design forms of evaluation adapted to demands in constant evolution (Barbot & Rivens Mompean, 2011, p. 56).

The self-learning course was first integrated into the curriculum in 2006. During its first edition, the course was restricted to students of English as a foreign language, but it was then broadened to the other languages mentioned above. The self-learning course's integration into the curriculum was based on three main objectives.

First, it was meant to be an opportunity for students to practically experience the theoretical notions they studied in other courses, such as learner autonomy, motivation and educational resources among others. This allows students a stimulating environment to build links between theory and practice (Korthagen & Kessels, 1999). For instance, having used OER for their self-learning, future teachers will be able to anticipate (some of) the difficulties their future learners will encounter using OER. Secondly, a self-learning environment allowed language teachers to deal with the great variety of language proficiency levels among students and to adapt each student's learning objectives to his/ her possibilities. Third, according to Germain and Netten (2004), learner autonomy is related to teacher autonomy. In consequence, the development of learner autonomy through the self-learning course is meant to improve students' subsequent teacher autonomy (Cappellini & Eisenbeis, 2013). The validation of the course and its development are based on continuing action-research.

## 2.	Intended outcomes:
The development of learner autonomy

The main pedagogical objective of the self-learning course described in this case study is to develop students' learner autonomy while learning a foreign language. Holec (1981)[1] defines learner autonomy as the capacity of a learner to take responsibility for his/her learning process. In other words, autonomy is opposed to heteronomy, where pedagogical decisions are made by someone else (usually the teacher or the institution) and imposed on the learner.

Learner autonomy involves five stages:

---

[1]. The reader should refer to Little (2012) and Sockett and Toffoli (2012) for discussions about the relevance of this definition in today's learning society.

- *Determining the objectives* according to one's specific needs. This is usually done in terms of procedural knowledge or skills, with sentences such as "I want to be able to…" and not in terms of content knowledge.

- *Defining contents and progressions*, that is the materials, in our case OER, to be used and their organization in a sequence. Materials are not necessarily chosen only for the linguistic forms they address, but may also be selected according to the contexts in which the learner will have to communicate.

- *Selecting methods and techniques to be used.* This is linked to the learner's linguistic biography and especially how he/she previously learned foreign languages (see Section 4). However, learning methods can change during the learning process.

- *Monitoring the procedure of acquisition*, which means that the learner decides when to study and how much time he/she will dedicate to those studies. He/she also decides where his/her learning takes place.

- *Evaluating what has been acquired.* At this stage, the learner evaluates to what extent his/her results meet the initial pedagogical objectives he/she established. Porcher (2004) suggests that in the case of language learning, the most effective way to do this is by direct exchange with other speakers of the target language. Of course, the criteria for this evaluation must be chosen by the learner, according to his/her learning objectives.

To accompany students toward learner autonomy, there are two main general pedagogical principles we adopted in the design and development of the self-learning environment. The first principle is that self-learning does not mean to learn alone and without any structure (Holec, 1981; Rivens Mompean & Eisenbeis, 2009). Holec (1981) argues autonomy "is not inborn but must be acquired either by 'natural' means or (as most often happens) by formal learning, i.e. in a systematic, deliberate way" (p. 3). In fact, autonomy is not only opposed to heteronomy, but also to anomy, that is the lack of any support or structure for the learner to rely on. The second principle is that OER could be a tool for the development of learner autonomy. However, OER need to be of different types in order for learners to make the most of their different cognitive and learning profiles (Barbot & Camatarri, 1999). Moreover, learners need to learn how to *find* and *use* OER, which is at the center of learners' advisors' concerns in self-learning environments (Little, 2012).

## 3.	Nuts and bolts: The self-learning environment at Lille 3 University

Every student goes through different stages advised by a tutor (whose roles are summarized at the end of this section). First of all, the learner takes two tests: a placement test, such as Dialang, to know his/her current proficiency level in the foreign language, and a test to discover his/her learning profile, such as SILL. Then, the learner has an individual advising session with the tutor to establish his/her learning objectives and consider possible OER and possible learning strategies to attain these objectives (Holec, Little, & Richterich, 1996). On one hand, learning objectives are formulated in terms of real life skills and based on the possible future use of the language by the learner (Porcher, 2004). On the other hand, the choice of OER and learning strategies is based on the learning profile and the proficiency level. OER are indexed in a closed database similar to that of the Merlot website for world languages.

During the first week after the advising session, each learner organizes the possibilities emerged during the session into two learning tasks. Beside task progression, students decide the parameters of two final products they will deliver at the end of the semester. They also establish an evaluation scheme which the tutor will use to grade these products. The criteria of the evaluation reflect what each learner thinks is most important for his/her language learning.

After these first stages, learners start to work autonomously. Each learning session ends with learners writing an entry in a logbook about their learning activities. In the logbook, learners explain their learning strategies and the OER used and they reflect on their efficiency. Learners send their logbooks to the tutor, who will give advice about learners' choices and will ask questions in order to allow learners to analyze more deeply their practices. These questions are aimed at guiding learners' attention to OER learning affordances (Van Lier, 2004) and how learners could possibly "divert" or adapt OER to better suit their learning objectives and strategies (see Section 4). From a cognitive point of view, this "diversion", which is in fact a particular case of appropriation, has been studied in terms of "instrumental genesis" (Rabardel, 1995; Rivens Mompean & Guichon, 2013). Finally, as part of their self-learning, learners can also attach language productions to their logbook and ask the tutor for feedback.

Three times during the semester, the tutor organizes a "learning to learn" group session. During these sessions, learners share their learning objectives and learning strategies and how they choose, use and possibly divert OER. During the discussion, learners could discover new learning strategies from other learners and possibly decide to try these strategies. Moreover, when a learner explains his/her strategies, he/she can benefit from other learners' suggestions and comments.

At the end of the semester, each learner has an individual self-evaluation session with the tutor. During this session, learners evaluate if they attained their initial learning objectives, they summarize their learning process and how their metacognitive skills – i.e. their ability to analyze their learning practices – evolved. The final grade combines the grades of the two language productions, evolutions in metacognition showed in the logbooks and the final self-evaluation.

Concerning the roles in this self-learning course, students are led to take responsibility for each stage of the learning process (Section 2) and are provided with different types of scaffolding (Van Lier, 2004). Consequently, the tutor has many roles. First of all, the tutor has to find OER and organize them into a database, which is a sort of "upstream scaffolding" (Rivens Mompean & Eisenbeis, 2009). Second, the tutor helps learners to elaborate strategies to find and select OER. Third, the tutor is an advisor, suggesting learning strategies to make the most of OER. It is important to highlight that the tutor never makes a decision for the learner, who is always a free decision-maker. Fourth, the tutor is an expert in the foreign language, able to give feedback adapted to learners' needs (Aljaafreh & Lantolf, 1994).

4. In practice: An example of instrumental genesis of OER

In this section, we show an example taken from the self-learning process of Valérie[1], a learner of Italian as a second language in the first post-graduate year during the academic year 2011-12. Her mother tongue is French and she studied English (advanced level) and Spanish (intermediate level) as second languages. She also studied Italian in a classroom-based course during one year in her undergraduate curriculum.

The first of her two tasks is to plan a trip to Italy and more specifically to find and book a hotel in Rome. The product delivered at the end of the task is a phone message to the answering machine of a hotel. She finds OER to work on basic expressions, communicative situations and grammatical contents useful for her task.

At the beginning of her self-learning process, she searches for OER adopting a "deductive" approach to grammar. For instance, when she studies articles, she starts from the grammatical rule and then she does some exercises to memorize the rule. In her logbook, she records the reasons for her choice[2]:

> [...] The reason why I choose to learn using this [deductive] method is because in all the language learning experiences I had, I used this method. So, I did the same way from habit. [...] Personally, the only efficient method for me to learn a new language is just the deductive method (13/10/2011).

---

1. A pseudonym.

2. We translated the logbook from French.

However, a week later evaluations of what has been acquired lead Valérie to notice that results are not as good as expected, which brings a drop in motivation:

> [...] I feel that for now, the work I've done isn't fixed in my memory. So, I need to read again and again, many times what I did earlier and this takes lots of time. [...] I lack motivation even though learning the language itself really interests me (18/10/2011).

The observation of a lack of efficiency leading to a lack of motivation brings Valérie to the conclusion that she should try another learning approach. This is suggested during a group session, when another learner explains his "inductive" method, which Valérie is then willing to try for herself. This implies a different use of OER, visible when she studies interrogative adverbs. She does not use OER to read the rule and then to put it into practice in grammar exercises. On the contrary, she decides to start with exercises to formulate a hypothesis about the grammar rule. Then, she tests her hypothesis on other exercises. Only at the end, does she compare the rule she elaborated with an online rule. This inductive approach proves to be more effective for her:

> [...] Before studying interrogative adverbs, I was reproducing the way I was taught languages. However, I felt that by doing exercises I didn't memorize what I was learning. I was learning deductively, relying on the rule and then doing exercises. I tried the other way around, that is to learn in an inductive way, which I had never done before. [...] Changing my learning strategy, I discovered that my previous way to learn a language wasn't the only one. [...] By creating my own grammar rule, I acquired more knowledge than before, since my memorization seemed to be more complete and efficient. Before, at the end of each learning session, the most of what I studied was already forgotten, while now I remember each adverb even two days after (1/11/2011).

This shift from a deductive strategy to an inductive one represents a step toward learner autonomy for two reasons. First, the learner realizes that there is a variety of possible learning strategies to attain the same learning (in this case: grammatical) objective. Alternatives are obviously a necessary condition to operate pedagogical choices and therefore to practise learner autonomy (Jézégou, 2002) and more generally pedagogical innovation (Alvarez, Beaven, & Comas-Quinn, 2013). Second, the learner realizes that the same type of OER can become an affordance to learn in different ways. In other words, the learner develops an instrumental genesis of OER to attain her objective in a way more suitable to her profile.

5.　Conclusion

Through the sections of this case study, we showed one way among others in which OER could be a tool for the development of learner autonomy and more generally of a learner-centered pedagogy. We would like to underscore that the self-learning environment shown in this case study gathers many different features that could be separated and adapted to classroom-based language teaching (Eisenbeis & Cappellini, 2013). As for this case study, it aimed at showing a practical example of how the same type of OER can be re-used in different ways according to learners' needs and profiles. To make the most of OER, our research suggests that it is important for learners to be aware of and open to different ways of using them. The learner "autonomization" process (Little, 2002) is triggered by an observation of a lack of efficiency, which leads him/her to search for and find new pedagogical contents and methods. The process goes from a use based only on previous learning experiences toward a reasoned usage based on the student's learning profile and the learning affordances of OER.

Therefore, we think that the availability of OER is necessary but not sufficient for the development of learner autonomy. In fact, mediations are at the very core of this process. First of all, the mediation of the teacher/tutor has to make learners question their pedagogical choices in order for them to open to different possibilities. Second, the mediation of peers through shared practices allows learners to discover other ways to use OER. To facilitate awareness of different possible usages of OER, it could be useful to associate each OER in a database with descriptions by learners of how they used it, including the learning objectives and strategies. These descriptions would constitute a repository of Open Practice (OPAL, 2011, p. 12) associated to the OER database aiming at promoting learners' awareness of different possible pedagogical choices and usages, hopefully leading in the end to learner autonomy. Future action-research is needed on this point.

In conclusion, we agree with McAndrew, Scanlon, and Clow (2010) arguing that OERs are a part of the educational experience and that "release of content is a key enabler for other activities" (p. 2). OER and OEP are an opportunity to develop "learning to learn" skills in initial education and to prepare learners for lifelong learning. It is our belief that in the future, educational institutions will not only be implicated in certificating learning (Pantò & Comas-Quinn, 2013[1]), but that they should also have a central role in implementing and evaluating new forms of mediation. Without such mediations, only learners who are already autonomous will take advantage of the open education movement, which would mean to deepen the gap between learners. On the contrary, if educational institutions develop learners' autonomy, more learners will be enabled to efficiently use OER, which would be a real step towards the democratization of education.

6.   References

Aljaafreh, A., & Lantolf, J. P. (1994). Negative feedback as regulation and second language learning in the Zone of Proximal Development. *The Modern Language Journal, 78*(4), 465-483.

Alvarez, I., Beaven, T., & Comas-Quinn, A. (2013). Performing languages: an example of integrating open practices in staff development for language teachers. *Journal of e-Learning and Knowledge Society, 9*(1), 85-92. Retrieved from http://www.je-lks.org/ojs/index.php?journal=Je-LKS_EN&page=article&op=view&path%5B%5D=804

Barbot, M.-J., & Camatarri, G. (1999). *Autonomie et apprentissage. L'innovation dans la formation*. Paris: PUF.

---

1. "After the first decade of OER, the business model that seems to be emerging is one where the course is for free but certification is for fee" (Pantò & Comas-Quinn, 2013, p. 20).

Barbot, M.-J., & Rivens Mompean, A. (2011). Un master de formation d'enseignants-formateurs en effervescence. *TransFormations, 5*, 55-67.

Cappellini, M., & Eisenbeis, M. (2013). Apprendre à apprendre pour apprendre à enseigner ? Une étude des liens entre autoformation en langues en formation de formateurs et la mise en place ultérieure de dispositifs et pratiques autonomisantes. *Education et Formation*, e-300. Retrieved from http://ute3.umh.ac.be/revues/

Eisenbeis, M., & Cappellini, M. (2013). Quelles pratiques pédagogiques pour l'autonomisation des apprenants ? *Les Langues Modernes, 2013-1*, 74-82.

Germain, C., & Netten, J. (2004). Facteurs de développement de l'autonomie langagière en FLE/ FLS. *Apprentissage des Langues et Systèmes d'Information et Communication, 7*, 55-69. Retrieved from http://alsic.revues.org/2280

Jézégou, A. (2002). Formations ouvertes et autodirection : pour une articulation entre liberté de choix et engagement cognitif de l'apprenant. *Education Permanente, 152*, 43-53.

Korthagen, F. A., & Kessels, J. (1999). Linking theory to practice: Changing the pedagogy of teacher education. *Educational Researcher, 28*, 4-17.

Holec, H. (1981). *Autonomy and foreign language learning*. Oxford: Pergamon Press.

Holec, H., Little, D. G., & Richterich, R. (1996). *Strategies in language learning and use*. Strasbourg: Council of Europe.

Little, D. G. (2002). *Learner Autonomy and Second/Foreign Language Learning*. Retrieved from http://www.llas.ac.uk/resources/gpg/1409

Little, D. G. (2012). Two concepts of autonomy in language learning and their consequences for research. In L. B. Anglada & D. L. Banegas. *Views on motivation and autonomy in ELT* (pp. 20-26). Bariloche: APIZALS Asociación de Profesores de Inglés de la Zona Andina y Línea Sur.

McAndrew, P., Scanlon, E., & Clow, D. (2010). An Open Future for Higher Education. *Educause Quarterly, 33*(1). Retrieved from http://oro.open.ac.uk/21894/1/McAndrew-_Scanlon-Clow-EQ.pdf

OPAL. (2011). *Beyond OER. Shifting focus on Open Educational Practices*. Retrieved from http://duepublico.uni-duisburg-essen.de/servlets/DerivateServlet/Derivate-25907/OPALReport2011-Beyond-OER.pdf

Pantò, E., & Comas-Quinn, A. (2013). The challenge of open education. *Journal of e-Learning and Knowledge Society, 9*(1), 11-22. Retrieved from http://www.je-lks.org/ojs/index.php?journal=Je-LKS_EN&page=article&op=view&path%5B%5D=798

Porcher, L. (2004). *L'enseignement des langues étrangères*. Paris: Hachette.

Rabardel, P. (1995). *Les hommes et les technologies. Approche cognitive des instruments contemporains*. Paris: Armand Colin.

Rivens Mompean, A., & Eisenbeis, M. (2009). Autoformation en langues : quel guidage pour l'autonomisation ? *Les cahiers de l'ACEDLE, 6*(1), 221-244. Retrieved from http://acedle.org/spip.php?article2445

Rivens Mompean, A., & Guichon, N. (2013). From the development of online resources to their local appropriation : a case study. *Journal of e-Learning and Knowledge Society, 9*(1), 37-46. Retrieved from http://www.je-lks.org/ojs/index.php?journal=Je-LKS_EN&page=article&op=view&path%5B%5D=800

Sockett, G., & Toffoli, D. (2012). Beyond learner autonomy: A dynamic systems view of the informal learning of English in virtual online communities. *ReCALL, 24*(2), 138-151.

Van Lier, L. (2004). *The Ecology and Semiotics of Language Learning: A Sociocultural Perspective*. Dordrecht: Kluwer Academic Publishers.

Links

Dialang: http://www.lancs.ac.uk/researchenterprise/dialang/about

Grammar rules and exercises: http://www.edelo.net/italie/base.htm#Les articles, http://www.oneworlditaliano.com/grammatica-italiana/avverbi-interrogativi-esclamativi-italiane.htm, http://www.oneworlditaliano.com/esercizi-di-italiano/articoli-determinativi-indeterminativi-italiani.aspx and http://www.oneworlditaliano.com/corso-di-italiano/esercizi-corso-di-italiano/corso-di-italiano-15.aspx

Learner profile test: http://www.apprendreaapprendre.com/tests/index.php

Merlot database: http://www.merlot.org/merlot/materials.htm?category=2440&&sort.property=overallRating

OER basic expressions: http://www.loecsen.com/travel/0-en-67-2-8-free-lessons-italian.html

OER communicative situations: http://www.oggi-domani.com/site/tableofcontent.htm

SILL: http://www2.education.ualberta.ca/staff/olenka.Bilash/best%20of%20bilash/SILL%20survey.pdf

17 Using MOOCs in an Academic English Course at University Level

Ana Beaven[1]

Abstract

Courses in English for Academic Purposes (EAP) in higher education contexts often bring together students from different academic fields. For this reason, such courses tend to present materials that are sufficiently general to be relevant to all students. However, teachers often need to supplement their teaching with online materials that are relevant to the participants' specific areas of study. Although MOOCs have not been designed as supplements to English language teaching and learning, this case-study illustrates how they can in fact provide a very effective and highly motivating way of enhancing EAP syllabi by allowing learners to enrol in courses of their choice, and select the materials that are most relevant to their language acquisition needs. Compared with other unstructured materials found online (journal articles, podcasts, video-recorded lectures), MOOCs provide an ordered set of materials made available weekly, through which students can develop the macro-skills of reading, listening and writing. At the same time, by putting the onus of choosing what and how much to study on the participants themselves, MOOCs can encourage learner autonomy and responsibility, and offer ways of pursuing academic language learning after the end of the EAP course.

Keywords: English for academic purposes, EAP, MOOC, student autonomy, motivation, supplementary resources, OER.

1. Università di Bologna, Italy; ana.beaven@unibo.it

How to cite this chapter: Beaven, A. (2013). Using MOOCs in an Academic English Course at University Level. In A. Beaven, A. Comas-Quinn, & B. Sawhill (Eds), *Case Studies of Openness in the Language Classroom* (pp. 217-227). © Research-publishing.net.

1.   Context

Courses in English for Academic Purposes (EAP) aim to develop in the learners the specific skills and knowledge necessary to study in an English-speaking academic environment. However, the students within a group often come from a variety of fields, making it difficult for the teacher to provide audio/video and written materials which are specific to the field of study and therefore particularly relevant to the individual student. This difficulty is evident in the choice made in most published textbooks to remain sufficiently general in the topics proposed so as to address the majority of the students in a class. At the same time, it is precisely this choice that often makes published books unattractive both to students and teachers, and require, to be successful, a substantial amount of more relevant (to the learners) supplementary materials.

Today, the Internet provides language teachers, and specifically those teaching EAP, with a wealth of potential resources to enhance their teaching. Examples of these are open access academic journals as well as *iTunes U*, which can be a source of freely-available podcasts and videoed lectures provided by universities on myriad subjects, from Astrophysics to Zoology. Making learners aware of these resources can encourage learner autonomy and motivation. However, these materials are often unstructured, and students can feel overwhelmed by the sheer wealth of resources, finding it difficult to select the material, set themselves reasonable objectives or have the discipline to use these supplementary materials regularly.

MOOCs (Massive Open Online Courses) take this a step further, by providing whole courses for free (for the moment) to learners all over the world. At the time of writing, Coursera, one of the main providers of MOOCs, offers 339 courses from 62 universities to over three million learners. Although not specifically designed to teach foreign languages, they can be seen as invaluable resources to teachers of EAP.

This case-study illustrates how these MOOCs were used to supplement a course in English for Academic and Professional Purposes offered at the University of Ferrara, Italy, in 2013. The participants came from different areas of study, including Economics, Law, Biology, Physics, Architecture, Literature and Medicine. The aim of the course was to enable the students to develop their English language skills for speaking, listening, reading and writing, in view of further academic studies or work, or their future employment. It was a semester-long 50-contact-hour course usually requiring an additional 50 hours of self-study.

Although supplementary materials such as *iTunes U* podcasts, *TED Talks* or subject-specific academic articles were used in previous editions of this course, the advent of MOOCs for education presented new possibilities by offering more structured open resources for EAP. The primary objective was therefore to offer the students the possibility of working with well-designed academic materials in English that were specifically linked to their fields of study. An additional aim was that of evaluating the usefulness of these materials in the context of an EAP course.

2.   Intended outcomes

With such a varied group of students in terms of their academic areas of study, it was important to provide general academic language input, such as practising the skills of note-taking, summarising and data commentary, while at the same time enabling learners to develop their knowledge of the specific language of their field. Previously, students had been given indications of websites where they could find podcasts or video-recorded lectures that could be relevant to them but, left to their own devices, the students had tended to do little extra work beyond what was strictly required for the course. This was mostly due to the time required to locate useful supplementary materials, as well as to the demands in terms of time management made on very busy students. In other words, if the students were not given explicit deadlines to carry out tasks, or a structured list of specific materials they had to use, the weeks would easily go by without them having found the time to study supplementary materials.

However, MOOCs seemed to provide ideal supplementary materials for these students for a number of reasons:

- the offer has increased in the last twelve months to the extent that it is now possible to find courses on a huge variety of subjects;

- the courses can easily be found in the websites of providers such as *Coursera*, *Udacity* or *Edx*, to mention but a few;

- being courses and not only collections of resources, they provide a clear structure that is easy to follow week by week;

- the length of the courses is usually relatively limited (many under ten weeks), which make them ideal as supplements to a semester course;

- being open, the participants can choose to do as much or as little of the work as they wish. This means that they can dose the amount of work according to their availability, as well as to their interests and needs;

- they are free (for now – this may well change in the future);

- they provide opportunities to listen (to lectures), read (documents provided) and write (in the forums and by completing assignments) in English;

- they offer learners the opportunity of an authentic academic experience in English, and an insight into a different academic culture (be it American or British, or from any of the other countries in which the institutions offering the courses are based).

3.   Nuts and bolts

The EAP Course described in this study ran from February until early June. With the help of a questionnaire submitted during the first week, an initial review of the participants' awareness of the existence of online resources to help them develop their language skills was carried out.

From the survey it appeared that, out of 20 students present in the class, 19 had used online dictionaries, 13 had read publications and 10 had watched broadcasts in English, only 4 were aware of the existence of *iTunes U* and none had explored the possibility of enrolling on a MOOC. Following this survey, the participants were introduced to some supplementary resources – including MOOCs – they could use to develop their knowledge of the language specific to their field of studies, and were made aware of the need to take some responsibility for their own learning. They were asked to explore the Coursera website (see Figure 1) and search for a course in which they might like to enrol. They were advised to choose one related to their studies or future profession or, if none could be found, one of a topic they felt was relevant to them. They were told that there was no obligation on their part to do all the work that was required within the course, but were encouraged to choose to do what they felt would benefit their English the most. They were also made aware of the fact that most courses offer certificates of completion which could be used in the students' portfolios or CV. They were also asked to preferably choose a course that finished before the end of the EAP course. Fortunately, many of the MOOCs offered by Coursera that particular semester began in March, which fitted perfectly with the organisation of the language course. It may be a good idea in the future to check the start dates of MOOCs on the websites of the various providers in order to direct the students to those beginning at a convenient time.

Before they began their MOOC, the students were asked what they expected to obtain from doing such a course as part of their EAP training. Developing their English was mentioned by all the students, although the focus ranged from improving listening, reading, writing or speaking skills to expanding vocabulary specific to a field of study, and becoming more confident users of the language. Some also mentioned acquiring new knowledge: "I expect to be able to understand a lesson taken in English and to discuss with people about issues of my field of studies", or "I expect to acquire more skills in reading and writing in an academic context, and to expand my vocabulary".

Figure 1.   The Coursera home page, showing a selection of courses offered

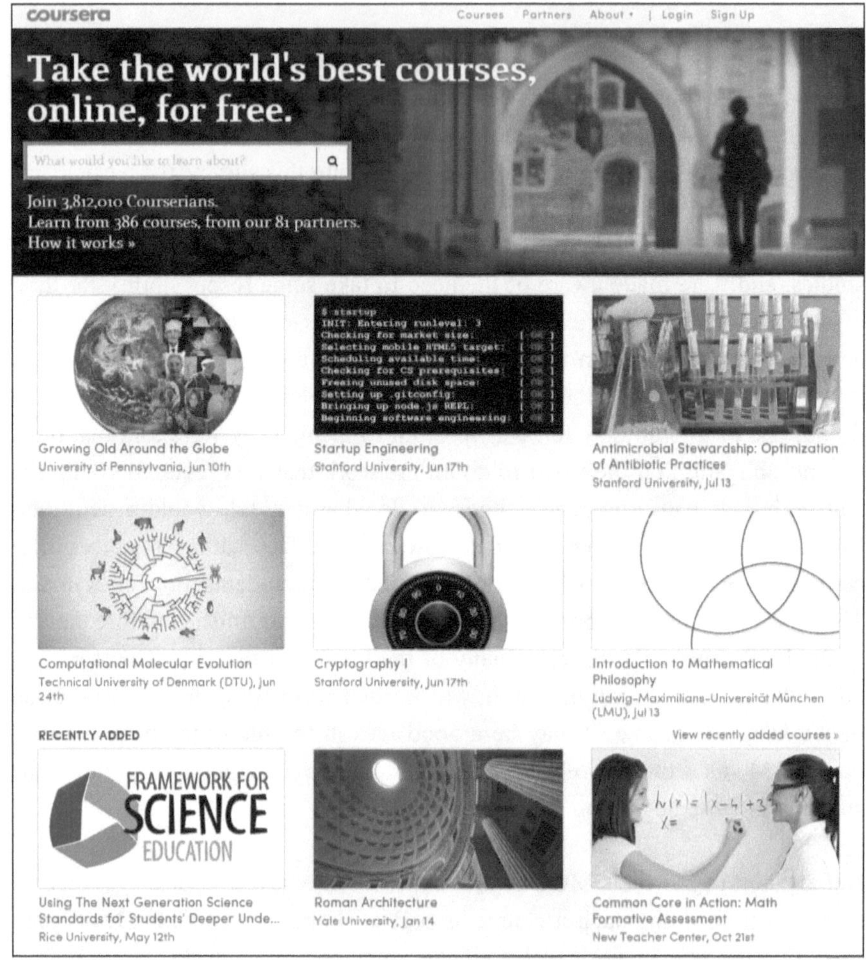

4.   In practice

All the students signed up for a MOOC on the Coursera website. The structure of the MOOCs and the open approach to learning imply that an underlying principle is the learners' freedom to do as much or as little as they wish. This is usually considered a weakness of MOOCs, leading to a putative high dropout rate. However, in this context, this aspect was undoubtedly a strength, as it enabled learners to select those parts of the course they found most useful to the development of their language skills.

Figure 2 below shows some of the courses that the students attended during the semester. It is clear that although most of the students chose courses that were related to their fields of study, others preferred MOOCs which offered the opportunity to explore new interests.

Figure 2.   Coursera MOOCs chosen by the students

Pay attention! ADHD through the Lifespan
Clinical Problem-Solving Neuroscience
Financial Engineering and Risk Management,
Foundations of Business Strategy
How Things Work
Genes and the Human Condition (from Behavior to Biotechnology)
Aboriginal Worldviews and Education
Introduction to Guitar
Know Thyself
Cardiac Arrest and Hypothermia
A beginner's Guide to Irrational Behaviour
Introductory Organic Chemistry - Part 1
Learn to Program: The Fundamentals
Learn to Program: Crafting Quality Code

In order to integrate the MOOC and EAP course more explicitly, and to ensure the students would pursue with their commitment, regular opportunities to exchange opinions and discuss learning outcomes were provided in class.

Discussions were also initiated in the EAP's Virtual Learning Environment (Canvas), where students were asked to tell each other about the courses they were doing. Figure 3 below is an exchange between some of the learners, showing how the fact of having to explain what the MOOC was about enabled students to reuse the vocabulary learned during the course.

Figure 3. An exchange between participants
and teacher on the EAP course's VLE

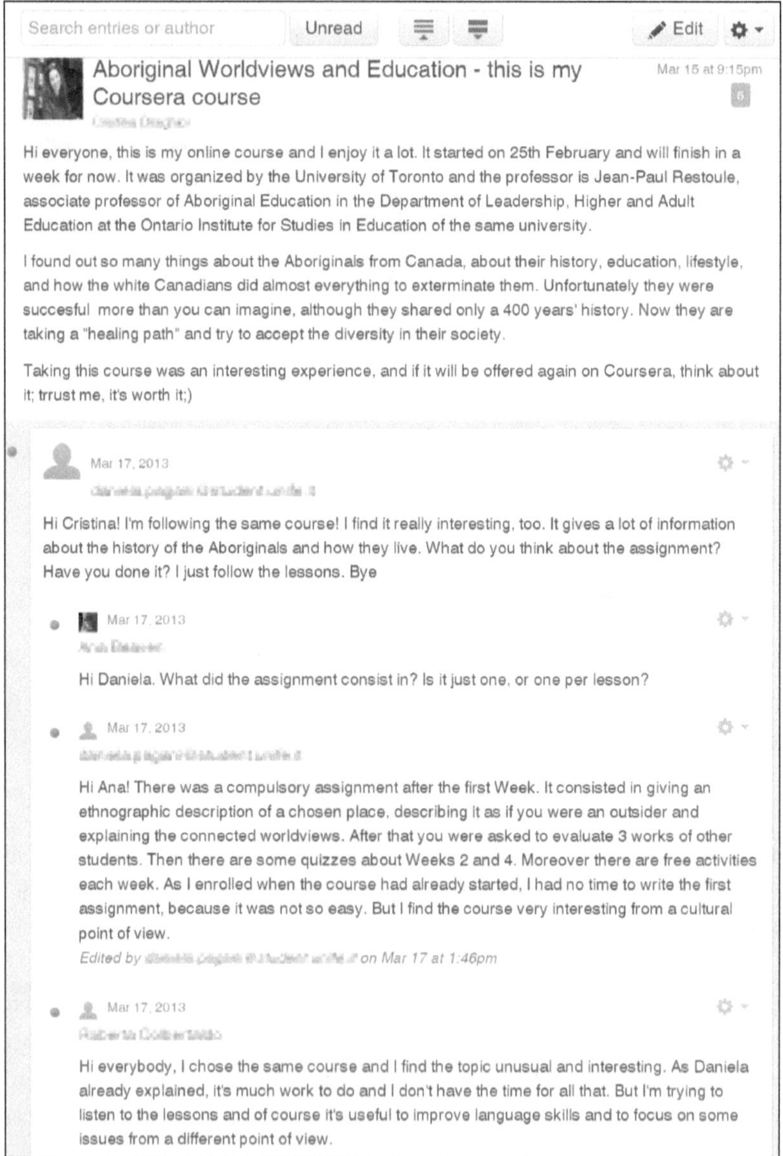

Similarly, towards the end of their EAP course, the students had the possibility of presenting the MOOC they had attended as part of a compulsory individual oral presentation task. Figure 4 below shows a slide from one of the presentations on the "Aboriginal Worldviews in Education" course offered by the University of Toronto.

Figure 4.　A slide from a student's presentation
of the MOOC she participated in

It is true that integrating a face-to-face EAP course with the experience of a MOOC implies that the teacher has no means of checking the activities that the students engage in. The extent to which the work done in the MOOCs is integrated in the EAP face-to-face course will depend on the individual teacher's preferences, the time available, and the context in which the course takes place. Some possible options include:

- regular in-class group discussions on the learning processes attached to the MOOC experience;

- writing tasks (such as reports, learning diaries, essays);

- student-led online discussions on the EAP's virtual learning environment (see Figure 3);

- oral presentations on the topic of the MOOC (see Figure 4).

Once they had concluded their MOOC experience, feedback was collected in the form of a questionnaire. It emerged that the dropout rate had been minimal, probably due to the fact that the students were given opportunities to discuss their learning in class, which may have functioned as regular motivation boosters. The students had also enjoyed being responsible for their own learning in terms of choosing what materials and sections of the course to study. This meant that, although by the standards of the MOOC providers, these participants may have been regarded as "dropouts" or unengaged students (some may not have watched the last video or done the last assignment, or done any of the assignments for that matter), they all felt they had been successful in their purpose of practising their English. In fact, all the participants declared they would recommend other learners of EAP to enrol on a MOOC in order to improve their English. When asked to give their reasons, they mentioned that it was "a funny and effective way to learn and improve English", and that the courses offered an opportunity to "improve a wide range of skills", including learning skills. One student pointed out that "lectures are given in a very clear English, it will be of help to anybody who wants to improve his/her listening skills and also learn something new in any field of culture and science. The choice is vast and the quality is great", while another mentioned that MOOCs offer "a unique opportunity to improve the language by listening to a native professional speaker, talking about a topic you feel motivated to know more about (or that you already feel comfortable with)".

Regarding the advice the participants would offer future students, this included choosing courses on topics of interest, even if they do not necessarily fit into the student's curriculum ("So do not choose a MOOC just because it fits their academic career at university, but because they think they could enjoy it"), to consider time-management carefully, ("take a long term course and take advantage [of peer-assessment]", "check what it requires in terms of assessment and workload") and ultimately, enjoy the course. Finally, all the participants declared they were very likely or almost certain to enrol on another MOOC in the future.

5. Conclusion

MOOCs have recently made their appearance in the higher education landscape and scholars, practitioners and administrators are trying to understand the different applications that this new type of course can have in the future. This case-study illustrates one valuable use – as support to English for Academic Purposes courses. It is arguable that the experience of MOOC inserted in a more structured course such as the English for Academic and Professional Purposes Course enabled the students to positively engage with this type of learning and increase their confidence in their own ability to benefit from Open courses in the future. In addition, it is to be expected that with the appearance of MOOCs in other languages (such as those promoted by the European consortium OpenUpEd), this resource will be available to learners of languages other than English.

Useful links

Canvas: www.instructure.com
Coursera: www.coursera.org
EdX: www.edx.org
OpenUpEd: www.openuped.eu
Udacity: www.udacity.com